LET THE PEOPLE CRY AMEN!

LET THE PEOPLE CRY AMEN!

by
John F. X. Sheehan, S.J.

PAULIST PRESS
New York / Ramsey / Toronto

ACKNOWLEDGMENTS

The excerpt from "Stopping by Woods on a Snowy Evening" is taken from *The Poetry of Robert Frost* edited by Edward Connery Lathem, copyright 1923, © 1969 by Holt, Rinehart and Winston, copyright 1951 by Robert Frost, and is reprinted by permission of Holt, Rinehart and Winston, Publishers. The excerpt from *The Once and Future King* by T. H. White is reprinted by permission of G. P. Putnam's Sons. The appendix of this book, tracing the sources of the Pentateuch, is taken from Martin Noth, *A History of Pentateuchal Traditions,* Bernhard W. Anderson translator, © 1972, pp. 261-276, and is reprinted by permission of Prentice-Hall, Inc., Englewood Cliffs, N.J.

Library of Congress
Catalog Card Number: 76-45676

ISBN: 0-8091-2003-8 (paper)
       0-8091-0217-X (cloth)
Cover Design: Tim McKeen

Published by Paulist Press
Editorial Office: 1865 Broadway, N.Y., N.Y. 10023
Business Office: 545 Island Road, Ramsey, N.J. 07446

Printed and bound in the
United States of America

Contents

To the members of the Company of Jesus
and their inspiration

"Master, go on . . ."
As You Like It
II.3.69

Preface

No teacher-administrator can continue to write without generous cooperation from a number of people. Prof. J. Coert Rylaarsdam read the entire manuscript and made suggestions. That these were sometimes ignored will be clear to the learned reader. Rev. Thomas Caldwell, S.J. read the manuscript and helped in many other ways, as did Rev. Patrick Walsh, S.J. At various times, research assistants Rita Burns, Carl Maxcey and Sandra Wackman made valuable contributions. Mrs. Lois Carlson performed many administrative tasks in her role as office manager and re-routed many others, thus freeing the author to write. Many of the re-routed burdens were then shouldered by Dr. Keith Egan and Rev. David Schultenover, S.J. I thank them for their generous help with chores, which took time from their own scholarship, and for their gifts of friendship.

Some of the chapters were written or outlined in Uppsala, Sweden, where I spent a happy semester under a grant from the American Council of Learned Societies. Many of the ideas in this book grew from dialogue in Uppsala with Prof. Helmer Ringgren and Dr. R. A. Carlson. I am grateful to them both.

No book was ever written on a university campus that did not owe much to students, graduate and undergraduate. I must thank all these students who have contributed much of the material that follows, criticized some of it, and challenged all of it.

The entire manuscript was typed (more than once) by Ms. Camille Slowinski, who worked with sturdy industry and resolute patience. These traits were much required by the author's penchant both for using neologisms and for discovering his own errors only when confronted with them in Ms. Slowinski's crisply typed pages.

Uppsala, Sweden—Milwaukee, Wisconsin   J. Sheehan
June 1974—April 1976

1
An Overview

One takes a risk in showing appreciation to a raconteur; he may proceed, then, to tell you another story. Such is the origin of this book. Its predecessor, *The Threshing Floor* (Paulist Press, 1972), has been received with extreme kindness by several audiences. These include the Roman Catholic audience in the college scene and outside of it, a clerical reading audience in the various Christian persuasions and a large number of Jewish lay people and rabbis. This sort of friendly response gives one the courage to try again.

How does this book differ from the first one? *The Threshing Floor* was designed with a stress on the theological and literary with an almost studious avoidance of the historical. The number of English language histories available, which treat the Hebrew scriptures well, is quite large. *The Threshing Floor* did not add to their number, nor will this work. There is, however, a significant difference between the two volumes. The first work alluded to the existence of "sources" in the composition of the Hebrew text. It frequently presupposed the validity of the scholarly judgment that the present Hebrew text is a compilation from these sources. However, it rarely examined the presupposition. Moreover, *The Threshing Floor* did not heed the evolutionary process of the textual development.

Let the People Cry Amen! will be quite different. In addition to treating a variety of themes not touched by the earlier work, the basic thrust of the work will be evolutionary. In dialogue with scholars and students, the author's acceptance of the scholarly judgment on the evolutionary nature of Old Testament theology is now more firm. Some gifted scholars are of other opinions, notably the Israeli, Y. Kaufmann, in his *History of The Religion of Israel* (in Hebrew), Tel Aviv, 1937-1956. Still, a good defense can be made for the hypothesis of evolutionary development. It is to be hoped that such a defense will be made throughout the book.

The consequences of this judgment are enormous. If a single page of Old Testament writing is a compilation of some sort from a host of sources, each of those sources can be a rich lode of insight into theological development. The thread of any single source can lead us to the discovery of the intense dialectic from which emerged the Old Testament as we have it. This is a most important point. Failure to grasp it can lead the reader of the Old Testament to find the pages dull and lifeless. An illustration may help. Modern films have made much use of "freeze-frames." The photograph remains some seconds on the screen. The viewer, who has seen the action that preceded the frame, understands that the figures in this picture are not lifeless; they are simply caught in a knife-edge moment. Like the figure on a Grecian urn, they are ever in movement while always at rest. Source criticism pushes this just a bit further. If we can tease out a single strand from a page, we can ask where this strand came from and what were the circumstances of its birth. For the reader who approaches the Old Testament in such fashion, the page becomes a means of getting in contact with centuries of theological ferment that lay behind the final compilation (which compilation for some texts may have been as early as 900 B.C.). The search for the backdrop of the ferment may bring the reader outside the nation of Israel and beyond the boundaries of Palestine. It is this search and its possible consequences that make source criticism worth the candle.

Dialogue with the Author

Sometimes readers view cynically the remarks of teachers stating that they have learned much from their students. That such learning is possible in graduate school and on the level of dissertation direction, most are willing to grant. Some have trouble in seeing that the dialogic process is a learning experience for the teacher on any lower level. But it is.

No matter how carefully a teacher may prepare his lecture material, no matter how sternly he may limit questions to a period at the end of the lecture, he will find the material considerably modified in the presence of an audience. If a good lecturer tape-records his lectures and then listens to them, he may find himself exclaiming occasionally not, "What a fine point!" but, "I wonder where I got it," so dramatic is the effect of the audience on his material. Obviously in dialogue after the lecture and outside of class, students may well educate the teacher further. This is obvious. What is not always so obvious is the effect that they have on him in the very presentation of the material.

Possibly this effect is really not mysterious. The concerned lecturer is always alert to facial expressions in the audience, to posture, to a variety of physical witness to the audience response of boredom, disbelief in the argument presented, or enthusiasm for it. Or it may be something more profound. In any event, it is a rare lecturer who does not find his material altered by the chemistry of censorship, editing, and re-phrasing which the audience thrusts on him.

This is, of course, an excellent education for the lecturer. The process, however, can also be an excellent education for the listener. In the ideal, the member of the lecturer's audience is not passive but dynamic. He asks himself questions constantly. At least in his own mind, he challenges the lecturer regularly. Were the lecturer to stop in the middle of a properly constructed paragraph, the listener ought to be able to finish the paragraph for him, or to show that the paragraph could not be finished—at least in the direction in which the lecturer was logically heading.

In the lecture situation, ideas change direction. Something that had seemed cogent in the unchallenged serenity of one's study seems far less compelling when presented orally to an intelligent audience. Moreover, even apart from the challenge of the audience, ideas have a life of their own, and it takes some time for them to live it out. Evelyn Waugh once remarked that in the writing of *Brideshead Revisited* one of his characters bothered him very much as she took form on the page. "She was behaving very strangely . . . I was relieved some days later to realize that she was an alcoholic." Any creative thinker will feel an affinity with this dynamic. Ideas are born, and the nature of their possible adulthood becomes clear only when they have reached a kind of adolescence.

Moreover, there is another dynamic afoot in the lecture method. One hearer may find a lecturer thrilling, and another hearer may find the same man tedious beyond description. And they may both be right. What popular parlance calls "personality" is something that students of metaphysics would call *relation*. It is something that exists between two. Consequently, when one of us finds another boring or captivating, we are saying something about ourselves as well as about the other.

Now how many of these dynamics can continue to operate on the printed page? In Mortimer Adler's classic of some decades back, *How to Read a Book*, the point was made that all these dynamics can operate for a reader. That they often do not operate is sad but avoidable. For the reader who becomes actively involved in reading a book, the problem of remembering what the author said is considerably lessened. One may have difficulties in remembering a conversation; it is almost impossible to forget an argument. The reader who actively challenges the author, who gets annoyed with him as he reads, who is alert to the author's inconsistencies as the reader sees them, can have little difficulty in remembering what the author said.

This is terribly important in reading a book on the Bible. In a subject this complex, any author is somewhat imprisoned by previous judgments. Perhaps in no field is it possible for a writer constantly to be re-thinking his positions on everything. After a serious amount of study in any complicated area, a writer reaches a conclusion. Subsequent conclusions will be limited by the first one. In a secondary area, the writer chooses from a number of possibilities that do not contradict a primary conclusion already reached. Obviously, there are points in his life when serious prior conclusions may be open to challenge. New data or new insights may force him to reappraise an original pre-judgment that imprisoned him somewhat. But this can happen only rarely in an academic career. The man with the absolutely open mind can solve only the simplest of problems. Life is too short to live this way.

But the reader ought to avoid being imprisoned by the author's pre-judgments. He ought first to divine what they are. The author may not express all of them directly, but their existence should become clear in one's reading. If the reader firmly rejects one or two of them, then sequelae that are acceptable to the author will not be acceptable to him. Still, if a number of conclusions seem to make sense in light of a larger picture, the reader may then want to challenge some of his own presumptions.

So presented, this may look somewhat abstract. In the course of the book, some of the author's pre-judgments will become clear, such as the already mentioned evolutionary nature of the Old Testament and the "cultic origin" of many Old Testament texts. The reader who challenges these views, who argues with them, who appraises what is written in terms of other possible mind-sets, who weighs carefully the possibility of other explanations for the conclusions that the author reaches, this reader will find himself truly in dialogue with the printed page.

Attitudes toward the Old Testament

If the reader so involves himself in the activity of reading, even objective mistakes by the author can enhance the learning process. Analogously, a variety of scholarly attitudes has been discovered to be compatible with a wide spectrum of religious attitudes. A stern insistence on the historicity of the biblical texts is compatible with deep religious faith or no faith at all. A conviction that the historicity of the Old Testament "does not matter" and that the major thrust of the work is to be found in its expressing a variety of themes—this attitude too is compatible with deep religious faith or its absence.

For some believers, the above may be difficult to grasp. (As some non-believers may feel compelled to cling to a dogma of unhistoricality.) As legend relates the words of the unlettered Joan of Arc, she was wiser than many believers. She was challenged by her inquisitors: "Those voices do not come from God; they come from your own imagination." To which she replied: "Of course, how else could God speak to me except through my imagination?" Many believers have not been so wise. They have confused truth and simplicity. In fact, truth is more often co-extensive with complexity. If, as Augustine remarked, a god that we can completely understand would not be God, so too a Scripture that we could completely grasp would be one that conveyed only little of his message.

Truth and Meaning

> The woods are lovely dark and deep
> But I have promises to keep
> and miles to go before I sleep
> and miles to go before I sleep.

Is this statement by Robert Frost *true*? Did the poet have a physical journey to complete? Is the possibility of a deeper meaning compatible with his description of a need simply to complete an actual journey?

The reader with some small experience in the reading of poetry may feel that these are terribly banal questions. But he has forgotten how many "clues" he has been given even before he reads the second line. He recognizes this work as "poetry" which, in contemporary American English, has its own set of rules in the manner of truth and meaning. Two or three thousand years from today, a reader with some grasp of twentieth-century American English will have many of the same difficulties in reading Frost that we have in reading the Old Testament. In other words, most of these difficulties are endemic to the Old Testament not as Scripture, but simply as written language.

The Title

The selection of a title for a book is not an easy task. I chose *Let the People Cry Amen!* for a variety of reasons. Most of them will be clear in a later chapter. This title was my second choice. My first choice was *The Qahal Learns and Teaches.* This title lost the competition, but it is a useful subtitle.

Qahal, of course, is the assembly of God, God's people gathered in worship or in proclamation of belief. The title was suggested to me by a percipient reader of the manuscript in an earlier version, who suggested that the great underlying theme of the book was not precisely consideration of Scripture, either Old Testament or New Testament. Rather, it was a portrait of God's people over a long history in the learning and teaching process.

The process began early in the second millennium before Christ. The *qahal* asked itself almost from the beginning: what is the significance of our new knowledge of the revealing God for the here and now? Even with the first meager knowledge of that God, the answer was not easy. How compatible is our new knowledge with what we always knew or what we are now learning about the present world? And while we strain and search for that compatibility, trusting only that it is there, *what do we tell our children?*

This bifurcation does not end with the close of the New Testament. The Scripture scholar is ever mindful of the temptations to *eisegesis*. The caution being noted, it seems difficult to read much of the Old Testament and New Testament without perceiving this dynamic so like the activity of the Church in our troubled age. This new knowledge that comes on us, some fret, makes things more complicated than they have been until now. Such knowledge does not illumine, as too much light blinds. And as new fragments of the theological puzzle are given to us, new insights in the world of the biological sciences, of sociology, of economics make new synthesis ever so difficult. What do we tell our children?

The answer to the modern question will be left to other books and perhaps to other authors. What concerns us here is watching the earlier *qahal* grapple with problems so very like our own. They did not always succeed. Nor shall we. Some efforts are worth more than certain attainments.

An overview of this kind ought not to be too long. Principles which may seem lifeless, viewed in the abstract, can show vitality when illustrated by specific problems. This much space was given to the first chapter for good reasons: The dynamics that govern the relationship between author-lecturer and reader-student are precisely the dynamics that operated in the *composition* of the Old Testament in its most primitive form. The Old Testament arose from a dialogue between authors and audience. With that in mind, it is easy to accept the judgment that a careful *reading* of the Old Testament involves not so much a meeting of minds as a meeting of persons.

Let the People Cry Amen!

2
My God, My Brother

Ah, but I was so much older then;
I'm younger than that now.

To perceive the emotional response of an audience to Bob
Dylan as he sings those words is to have an unusual experience.
The proper audience for Dylan, those who entered the more
serious phases of adolescence in the early sixties, finds the impact of these and similar verses to be overwhelming. Dylan is
one of them. What he articulates, they feel mutely but really.
What he prophesied a decade ago in the matters of war and
peace, brotherhood and ecology, his audience feels has come to
pass. Many of his verses, then, touch off an enormous emotional charge, bringing to life for a moment a decade that is
gone.

One may ask, how much of this emotional charge will be visible on the printed page in fifty years. The evocative melodies
are beautiful, of course, and they may help to reconstruct the
force that Dylan had on an age. But even with devices of recording and films, can the emotional impact easily be brought
to life? Or will Dylan present the puzzle to a later age that
poets of another era offer to us? We read Thomas Hood's material and ask ourselves how an intelligent audience could have
loved him so. The problem, of course, is that no matter how we
may insist on the intrinsic merit of the printed word, any printed material was at one point composed for a particular audience. A most serious dimension of the meaning of that written
material is possible for us only if we can recapture some of the
mood of that earlier audience. The audience of the Old Testament fluctuated considerably over the twelve hundred years

or more of its composition. Is it possible for us to capture the mood of those fluctuations to some extent?

It probably is possible, since the Old Testament is, on one level, such a human project. Humans find thinking hard work. Most of us engage then in serious thought only if we are confronted with greater pain for failure to think. The pain of an unresolved problem must be greater than the pain of trying to solve it. If we seriously search the solutions that a given "source" in the Old Testament touches on, we can come to understand the nature of the problems faced by that source. Reading extrabiblical materials that are contemporaneous with a given Old Testament source, we may touch on a problem that the Old Testament felt demanded a solution. By coming to an appreciation of this dialectic, we can come to some feeling for the mood of the Old Testament audience.

This sort of "challenge and response" dialectic is hardly limited to the Old Testament. Roman Catholic priests who finished their studies in the past decade may never have been seriously exposed to the question of *Milleniarism* (a "thousand year" reign of the Messiah at the end of the world). In most seminaries in the Roman Church the issue never came up. It was not defended, not attacked, but ignored. In many contemporary Protestant seminaries the issue was a lively one. So different were the pressures on these two Christian groups living contemporaneously in one society.

But the circumstances surrounding a community that thinks may not only affect the problem to be solved, but may become part of the solution. Most successful thinking communities mingle charismatic insight and cultural conditioning in the solutions they offer. In the Roman Church, the documents of Vatican I (1870) offer a basically humble teaching on papal authority. They declare that the pope teaches "with that infallibility which is proper to the Church." The nature of such infallibility is not further proclaimed. Should the infallibility be later described as limited, or even nonexistent, the core proclamation of Vatican I would remain intact. So did the charismatic insight of the assembled fathers express itself.

The cultural conditioning is to be found, however, throughout the document. If one listens carefully, one can almost hear the sound of trumpets. Asking the question, "What does authority itself mean?", the assembled fathers look at the monarchies around them, threatened, under attack and being extinguished. Overcome with nostalgia, they gaze fondly back at a past that had perhaps never existed. They think of a perfect monarchy as the ideal authority and so describe the papal office. Among all these trees, the forest of a humble view of papal authority is easily lost to view. The serious student of theology, dealing here with a document that is only a century old, deliberated on by moderns and written in a Western language, must work hard to find the kernel of truth in a cultural husk. The student of the Old Testament, dealing with material that is ancient and Semitic, must work even harder.

But one may ask a further methodological question. Even if it is possible to delineate the dominance of one problem-idea in the growth of the Old Testament, is it possible so to delineate the movement from one idea to the next as to write a "history of ideas" for the Old Testament that is truly evolutionary? It probably is possible within limits, but an evolutionary history of Old Testament thought with clearly marked beginning, middle and end, might be suspect. Thought does not move so neatly. Moreover, in matters of the Old Testament, one must always distinguish between the reality of the Old Testament life as it was lived—and as it was recorded.

The Patriarchal Period

Before looking at the religious insights of this period, we must confront a recurring problem in Old Testament studies— the "historicality" of a given era as the Old Testament records it. The significance of concluding that something is historical or non-historical ought not to be exaggerated. The world of religious literature, in and outside the Judaeo-Christian tradition, is filled with examples of profound religious teaching communicated through the medium of fiction. Still, there are several modes of communicating historical truth. One ought not to move too quickly from the Old Testament's use of a mode unfamiliar to the modern West to the conclusion that the Old Testament is non-historical. As so frequently, here also, one must pay heed to the *literary form* used. Would the following little story, for example, be incomprehensible to a young Western reader:

> There was once a mean old lady named Brittania. She had two sons, Canadus and Americus, and as they grew older they resolved to settle their differences with her. They went about this in their own separate ways. . . .

Although this literary form is not common in the modern West, it takes little imagination to see that a history could be written this way. The history might lack a certain amount of nuance. It might, however, not be much less nuanced than most history that is studied on the pre-college level.

Some scholars feel that much history in the Old Testament is presented in this fashion. They call the figures in this writing *eponymous ancestors*. A given name, Abraham, Isaac or Jacob, becomes the focus for the history of an entire people. Complicated events, such as the migrations of nations, are described in the movement of a clan chieftain.

A parallel to the Old Testament use of eponymous ancestors (if it is such) can be found among Arab legends. These tend frequently to subsume the events of tribal life into the activity of one great sheikh. If this is a valid parallel, it would be another example of the manner in which the life-style of the ancient Hebrew lives on in that of certain of the modern Arabs.

What are the advantages of this literary form? For most people, it is entertaining. It moves history from the realm of study to storytelling. If details are lost in the shift, the likelihood that the broad pattern will be easily memorized is much enhanced. Moreover, it becomes infinitely more personalist. Some of us might have difficulty in empathizing with an ancient nation that feared extinction as a nation (but could easily continue to live on merged with other national groups). But who of us cannot feel the anguish of an aging married man who does not have an heir? This personalism is a terribly important facet of Old Testament history, since the function of that history was largely to assure a national identity. The overwhelming majority of the persons who constituted Israel in Solomon's time— even more so those of the later epochs—had little blood relationship to the heroes of the patriarchal age. (Even as most Americans alive today stem not from the Revolutionary War but from the immigration of the nineteenth and twentieth centuries.) If history was to unify, these later Hebrews had to be able to identify with the early national origins. The intense personalism of this type of history-writing helped to make it possible. It has often been noted that America's Blacks have had great difficulty in so empathizing with America's Revolution as to feel themselves somehow a part of it (as most immigrants have succeeded in doing, although they arrived long after the Blacks). It is intriguing to speculate that the Blacks might have identified easily with the American Revolution— with enormous consequences for American national unity—if the literary mode featuring eponymous ancestors had been in use in the modern West. So presented, the Revolution would have been personalized as the struggle of a single suffering man. With this man the Blacks might easily have felt a strong common bond.

Within the framework of a historiography that differs from our own, there is much evidence for a historical fundament to the patriarchal narratives. The narratives fit into an emerging pattern of national migrations contemporaneous with the patriarchal period. As has often been noted, details are found in the patriarchal narratives, verified by extrabiblical texts discovered in our modern era, which could have survived in ancient Israel only in connection with sagas faithfully transmitted from a more distant time and place. Names appear in the patriarchal narratives which have proved to be genuine in the flavor of the locales in which the Patriarchs were said to be moving. Such details are of even greater significance, since, as far as we can see, the Old Testament is not interested in proving its veracity. What proofs it offers seem to arise by accident.

Also supporting the historicality of much of the Old Testament is the manner in which the accounts treat what Brandeis scholar Nahum Sarna has called their "inconvenient" Babylonian origins. The origins are inconvenient because the Hebrew people are to make such a strong demand on their claim to Canaan. It is inconvenient to their argument to admit that at a time when other peoples were well established in Canaan, the core of the Hebrew nation arrived as immigrants, took other peoples to themselves but put their stamp on them, and then dominated the land. It is "inconvenient," but it is true and so it is recorded.

The "Pietas" Dynamic

Still, if the Old Testament shows scruples in the matter of historicality of events, there is probability that these scruples are occasionally overcome when recording the theology of an earlier epoch. For example, the Old Testament tends to present the early heroes and heroines as monotheists, although some details which are transmitted (generally in connection with a good story) lead us to suspect amounts of polytheism in the ancient Hebrew world (*Gen.* 31:19-35). Though the details are left intact, their theological significance is frequently bleached out from the epic. One might call this the *Pietas* Dynamic.

Pietas has a threefold dimension in Latin. (The term is advisedly left in Latin, lest it become confused with the word *piety* in English.) One of the three dimensions of the Latin word has to do with the feelings that dutiful children have for their parents: loving, reverential, kind. The virtue is demanded mostly in the old age of one's parents. Even in societies that do not admit of easy upward mobility for the young, elderly parents find themselves eventually inferior to their children—physically and intellectually. The son and daughter, gifted with *pietas* now reverse the familial procedure and deal with their elders as parents deal with very small children; they make very few demands; they ignore much "misbehavior"; they explain much in terms of weakness.

It is easy to see something like this afoot in the common psyche of the Hebrew people. They look back fondly to the activities of Abraham, Isaac, and Jacob as to the activities of beloved—but aged—parents. They try to depict them in the colors of a purified religion of a much later time. Still, some of the footprints of an earlier type of religion are left undisturbed in the accounts. For example, the patriarchs made frequent use of *masseboth*. In fact that word refers to "idols"; the word commonly has that meaning in other Semitic languages. Sometimes the Hebrew editor adds a qualifying phrase which disguises the old meaning (as in Exodus 24:4 where Moses is said to raise "pillars" to the memory of Israel) and sometimes not. This is one of the things that makes the Old Testament difficult reading.

For the believer, this kind of discussion could be consoling. Though the mode of writing history in the Old Testament (and in the ancient Near East) is different from our own, it is a valid mode. Although the Old Testament apparently did not intend to prove its veracity, it frequently does just that by showing its heroes with warts and all. Still, religious communication does not always need strict history (consider the parables in the New Testament). Spared the need of poring over the texts and searching for literary forms that they frequently do not contain and a kind of history that they generally do not offer, the believer will find himself more open to that proclamation with which the Old Testament concerns itself.

Hebrew Religious Genius

It is often said that the Hebrew people were possessed of "spiritual genius." Sir Flinders Petrie, the late great Nestor of modern archaeology, used to explain much of his success in finding valuable artifacts by a single intuition. He studiously avoided Hebrew sites and searched the areas of their contemporaries. The "people of the book," he felt, were simply not interested enough in material goods to have left rich treasures behind. His intuition was rewarded. Still, the nature of this "spiritual genius" needs to be delineated. It cannot be compared with the metaphysical insights of Greece's golden age in philosophy. It was not totally original. The nature of the Hebrew insight was its ability to come on a theological truth in the hands of contemporaries and to retain it after the contemporaries had passed from the scene. In some cases, the contemporaries remained, but they lost their original insight.

It is possible for a nation to lose an insight in a variety of ways. Perhaps common to all of them is the failure to share the insight by the entire community. It does not suffice that a small circle of the intelligentsia should have an insight. They must communicate it to a relatively broad circle if the idea is to live. It is theoretically possible, of course, for a small gnostic circle to exist in an unknowing larger group, to find within each generation a select body of disciples and to indoctrinate them. Practically, however, this presents difficulties. The larger body must be somewhat accepting of the ideas, if only to provide the smaller core of initiates. More than once in history, a religious insight died for lack of the larger body to provide the inner core. But many insights continued to live as the idea moved from the originators to the Hebrew people.

The Divinity as Person

Were the patriarchs monotheists or even henotheists? (If the latter, they would have believed in a single powerful deity while yielding to a kind of agnosticism on the limitations suffered by certain lesser deities.) A developed answer to this question can await another chapter. Here it can at least be admitted that the patriarchs suffered a certain ambivalence on this point. To dispute the degree of monotheism shared by the patriarchs is to lose sight of one great religious insight they did have. They came to have an appreciation of the Divinity as person and as loving person. And they manifested this appreciation in a variety of ways.

The first way—and perhaps the clearest—was in their use of special names for the Divinity. One sometimes reads that modern Western society does not have anything comparable to the

Old Testament use of names. (Although some might cite the "litanies" of the Roman Church.) Still, we do not have the totally magical view of names that the ancient Near Eastern world had. We do not feel that to know the name of a thing is to be able to control it. We do not see immediately (as the Eastern legend does) that Adam could prove his superiority to the angels, since he knew the names of all the beasts and they did not.

And yet, is the "magical" view of names totally without parallel in our society? Do not most of us have a name that only one or two persons in the whole world may use in addressing us? Certainly, there are names that are so intimate or so jocular that their acceptable use is quite limited. The person who may use a particular name for us may not "control" us with magic force. Still, he surely has a kind of influence on us that other persons do not have. The name that this person may use at least symbolizes the relationship. There may be periods in our lives when the name may even cause the relationship, if only by reminding us of a relationship that once was and that the name causes us to honor still, although we feel that relationship now to be largely dead.

So did the patriarchs deal with the Divinity. Each had his own special name for the God. He is frequently cited as the God of Abraham, Isaac and Jacob, the God of the father (my father or your father), but he is also cited by particular names to describe his relationship with each of the three great patriarchs. Each of the names has a special significance of its own, derived from the meaning of the name, even as the use of the "special names" in our own language has a role to play in describing the relationship. Such names tend to describe the degree of intimacy or friendship, the "social superiority" of one or the other of the two persons in the relationship. But in the world of the Old Testament, apart from the studied significance of each of the names, the fact that the names existed was itself of significance. The Divinity was at one and the same time the God of Abraham, Isaac and Jacob and that Divinity who was greeted by special names used, apparently, by the patriarchs as they addressed the Divinity.

For the patriarch, it was deeply comforting when he prayed

that he addressed "the God of my Father." As so frequently in the Old Testament world, this enabled the worshipper to approach the Divinity not as a stranger, but as "family." The patriarch realized that he stood in a long, traditional chain of worshippers of this Divinity, that his predecessors had been faithful to the Divinity and their faith rewarded, that the relationship he was entering with this Divinity was not something brand new.

And yet each of the patriarchs had his own name for the Divinity. Before commenting on those names, one can note that one observation on this practice of double-naming the Divinity is quite consonant with the biblical text. The patriarch worships the God of the fathers. He never rejects the God of the fathers. He prays confidently to the God of the fathers as his God. And yet, he comes to have his own special name for the Divinity, a name at least symbolizing his own special, personal relationship with the Divinity. It is tempting to suggest that what lies behind this is the adoption of a special name for the Divinity in one's maturity, not ignoring the idea that this Divinity is He Who is the God of the father, but confessing that he is also *my* God and that his relationship with me is now best expressed by a special name.

We are told that the Divinity is the shield (*magen*) or the suzerain (*magan*) of Abraham. The only difference between these two being in vocalic spelling, a strong case can be made for either, since Old Testament scholars generally feel more confident about the consonants in Old Testament Hebrew spelling than they do about its vowels. In either case, Abraham saw the Divinity as protector (in a world in which a man sorely needed protection). If the latter interpretation is correct, Abraham's use of this name implies a covenant relationship between the two of them. At the core, then, of Abraham's dealings with the Divinity was his obligation to serve that Divinity in a variety of ways, externalizing his love, while realizing that the Divinity did not need his service. Isaac's name for the Divinity is a bit more revealing. For him the Divinity is the "fear" or "kinsman" of Isaac (*pahad*). The meaning of the word is not clear in Hebrew. It can be related to a common

Hebrew word meaning "fear," but most scholars tend to look to the other Semitic languages to explain its meaning. Cognates show the word to have the meaning of relative or family member, "thigh" (a common Semitic euphemism for the male sexual organs), the sexual power. In our world, which has largely desacralized sex, effort must be made to see this as the Hebrews saw it. Assuredly part of their esteem for sex rested in the desire to have descendants and a certain immortality through them; part of the esteem (manifested in ancient fertility cults) flowed from an appreciation of the need for a regular —and fruitful—sexual activity, if the living world were to survive. But part of it in later Jewish thought (with some antecedents among the ancient Hebrews?) flowed from the acceptance of sex as something that led a man out of himself and gave him a taste of the transcendent. It was this last that enabled later Jewish writing to answer its own question, "With the destruction of the temple in Jerusalem, where did the Spirit of God take up residence?" in the following manner: "Thereafter, the Spirit of God was found in two places, in the schools where learning takes place and in the embrace of a man with his wife." The sacredness of learning and family were to become the pillars of later Judaism. At least one of these two pillars may trace its sacred status back to the patriarchal period.

Against the above, it becomes easier to define Jacob's special name for the god of the fathers. The name can mean "mighty one" or "bull" (*'abir*). There is much to be said for the latter, of course. Not only does it fit with the general importance of sexual prowess in a religious context from this period, but bull worship was a terribly important part of the world in which Jacob lived. Here then the patriarch would, understandably, have combined the God of the father with a vital aspect of Divinity as it was seen in the world around him.

Aḥam-arši

In the Babylonian world contemporaneous with that of the patriarchs, a number of names for the Divinity are used that combine the names of son, father and brother with some other component. Despite the world around them, which saw divinities largely as forces and not persons, despite a world which saw these forces as threatening and punitive, some ancient theologians were more insightful. They saw a Divinity as somehow "family" and consequently hailed him, "my God is father," "my kinsman is el," or "my brother-god is help." Finally, one pious worshipper exultantly named his Divinity, "I have obtained a brother!" (Aḫam-arši) "I am not alone in this world. I have a Divinity with whom I can have a relationship of familial intimacy." This was the insight seized on and preserved by the ancient patriarchs.

Doubtless the patriarchal period is replete with other insights, and some of them are recoverable from the Old Testament text. This one alone is a major contribution: that the Divinity is not simply a powerful force but "family," and that he may be approached with that confidence with which one approaches a beloved brother.

3

Oral Composition
and Literary Criticism

In the judgment of many scholars, a long history of oral composition lies behind the earliest written forms of the Old Testament. Scholars differ considerably in their judgment about the amount of the finished product that began in the oral stage. They also differ in their speculation on the precise manner of this oral composition, but that there is an oral component to the Old Testament text is beyond dispute. To a certain extent, of course, any composition is oral. Careful writers show concern for the sounds of the words used in any written composition. A contemporary of James Joyce quotes him in answer to the eager question, "What advice would you give a young writer?"

When you write, you must listen for sounds.
And there is a sound that one word makes
and there is the sound that one word makes upon another
and there is the sound of silences between words.

In an infinitely more complicated manner, Joyce expresses the same thought in *Finnegan's Wake* in a pair of typically Joycean sentences replete with puns of sound and spelling to prove his point. (Cf. *Finnegan's Wake*, p. 482 and the sentence that begins, "That's the point of eschatology. . . .")

But there is far more to "oral composition" of the Old Testament than that it is oral as all composition is oral. There is steadily emerging evidence that at least certain areas of the Old Testament show layers of composition that were totally oral, that repetitive formulas are used not only because the composer liked the sound of them, but because he needed them as a memory device. (After all, long before the printing press had weakened the demands that society felt it could make on the memory, Augustine referred to the memory as "that treacherous treasure-house!") Finally, studies done in fairly recent years have led to the conclusion that an analogous type of composition has gone on in our lifetime, and that by studying this fairly contemporary material, we can come to some understanding of the Old Testament, whose origins are hidden from us by millennia.

The oral dimension of Old Testament composition was among the sensitive themes treated by a Roman Catholic priest publishing in 1678, Fr. Richard Simon. Coming from a rich background in ancient literatures—which he had been able to study with relative serenity—he published a three volume work on biblical studies and found himself the center of great controversy. Actually, his insights were basically modest as viewed in our time, but well ahead of his age. He suggested that Moses was not *tout simple* the author of the Pentateuch, that the Old Testament had been composed in a rather complicated fashion, and that much oral composition lay behind the earliest written stages of Old Testament composition.

His insights fell on barren soil. The great names in the Roman Church greeted his ideas with hostility. Even the notion of a modest complexity in the composition of the sacred texts was attacked with ferocity. The harm that these attacks accomplished by their savagery was enormous. No one could reasonably object to the idea of disputing with Simon. In fact, it is the thesis/antithesis movement that normally leads to scholarly synthesis. But the warmth of the attacks and the authoritarian strictures that were laid on Simon caused many of his ideas to lie infertile in the Roman Church for centuries.

For some of his ideas, this was only mitigated tragedy. Some of his suggestions, which did not fructify in the Roman Church, led to new growth elsewhere. But his views on the vital oral component of Old Testament composition lay largely dormant for two and one-half centuries. Only with the emergence of the

"Uppsala School" in twentieth century Sweden did these ideas return to life. While many would reject the extent to which the Uppsala School uses oral composition to explain textual problems, there is no dispute on the general usefulness of an oral composition hypothesis. Serious study of this hypothesis and its limits was delayed for centuries by partisan religious attack. A high price was paid in the name of a religious homogeneity.

Complexity of Composition in the Ancient World

Part of the difficulty that some have in separating sources from one another on a given page of the Old Testament flows from a failure to understand some of the major differences between composition in the modern West and the ancient East. Some of the most serious differences are found precisely in the use that ancient authors made of sources. "Plagiarism" is an ugly word in the West. The modern author makes serious efforts clearly to identify every line and every idea that is not totally his own. The ancient author, even in the West but especially in the East, is not so bound. In fact, he has some obligations that compel him in an opposite direction. Since the totally original is highly suspect in the ancient East, the author is compelled to use material from his predecessors; he is obligated to certain stylistic devices and clichés. The ancient composition grows then through a process of accretion. The original, new and exciting is added to the existing, old and familiar. This method is not peculiar only to the East (witness Vergil's use of Homer), but it did not live on in literature to modern times. Perhaps the only modern Western parallel is the obligatory use of clichés in films. There is a certain type of "contemporary modern" in films that seems almost as obligated to clichés such as slow motion and sepia tinge shots as the ancient author was to a variety of stylistic devices, motifs and choice of themes.

Because of this commitment to the past, the final redaction of the work did not always produce a homogeneous mass. Rather, the end product can usually be resolved into the original components. This is so, not only because of the stark differences in the original components (which will be discussed further in this chapter), but because of the final redactor's compulsion to show respect for the material, whether written or oral, that had preceded him and that he used in creating his own literature.

Oral Composition Today

One phase of the oral composition dynamic still lives among us. Biographers of Martin Luther King note that one special phenomenon asserted itself in his preaching and speaking after the famed March on Washington. Frequently thereafter in his public addresses, whether his topic was peace in Vietnam or honest wages for sanitation workers, a special few paragraphs might appear at the end of a given speech. With a few transitional sentences, sometimes graceful, sometimes not, Dr. King would begin something the crowd had secretly hoped for. He would throw back his head, close his eyes and proclaim: "Brothers and sisters, I have a dream! . . ." And the crowd would explode as he paraphrased his own previous speech, describing his vision of the future in rich, biblical cadences, with descriptions of the leveling of hills, the filling of valleys and— more miraculous yet—the loving union of Black and White in a peaceful America.

Some of Dr. King's friendly biographers are embarrassed by the audience reaction. It strikes them as too closely parallel to the reaction of a crowd when a popular entertainer begins the opening verses of one of his old favorites, a song "hit" of the past or a "routine" with which he has long been associated. At this point, crowds frequently applaud even as he begins. They are, it has been noted, applauding not so much the entertainer as they are applauding themselves and their past memories the introduction brings to mind. Audience reactions to Dr. King and to popular singers have been similar. But is it embarrassing? Only to those who do not understand the centuries-old role that audience reaction has played in oral composition of religious literature. Any religious leader must be—in part—entertainer. No religious leader can lead effectively who routinely bores his audience unto pain. Consequently, even in a modern and literate society, the themes to which the leader returns and the mode in which those themes are expressed are largely determined by audience reaction.

Because of the widespread literacy in America and because of the faithful recording in sundry ways of virtually every word that Dr. King spoke in public, the second phase of oral composition did not occur. In this phase, the faithful disciples recreate from memory the words of the cultic leader or prophet and rearrange them in a variety of orders. Thus the "school of Isaiah" may have rewritten much of the earlier material so that large measures of the entire work are seen colored by the vision described in chapter six of Isaiah. For this reason it is pointless to question (as some scholars do) whether or not this vision took place at the beginning of his prophetic career. The school of Isaiah, properly, saw the vision as bathing all the great prophetic teaching, no matter when it occurred. (Had King's works been so assembled, "I have a dream! . . ." would have colored everything else he ever wrote.)

This second phase of oral composition is not operative in our society. But since the first phase is still quite operative, it is easy to understand the entire dynamic. One of the delicate functions, then, of literary criticism is to tease out, when it can be done with any degree of accuracy, those portions of the final compilation that can be seen as clearly oral. Finally, it may be noted here that the primary phase of oral composition is not something to be limited to the material that is gathered in the final compilation under the rubric of "prophetic" writing. There is evidence that much narrative material in the Old Testament is composed under cultic auspices, and there is some evidence that the cultic leader was encouraged to speak freely in parts of the cult. (For example, so may be interpreted the verses in Exodus 20:19, where Moses is encouraged to deliver God's message to the assembly. "But do not let God speak to us, lest we die!" Some scholars see here the foundation of a rubric that allowed the Hebrew religious leader to speak freely at the close of a cultic ceremony, but to speak freely *as though speaking for the Divinity*.)

"Qahal" as Creative Censor

Our largely democratic society does have difficulty in understanding one aspect of the oral composition process, at least
until this aspect is spelled out a bit. The *qahal* (religious assembly) of the people has a vital "input" into the final composition. A democratic society sometimes has difficulty in understanding the spectrum of ways in which persons can have
influence. Negotiation between equals is one way of fulfilling a
common effort toward agreeing on a truth, religious or other. It
is, of course, not the only way. The Greek Church today understands this well. It speaks of *pleroma* (the general consensus)
as the criterion for the mainstream of church teaching. Something mildly analogous to this was present in the example from
Dr. King's preaching. The audience response of tears, ap-
plause, and cries of "Amen!" was influential in keeping certain
portions of the King teaching prominent in the corpus of the
works that he regularly delivered. Other portions, which were
not so endorsed by the audience, passed from the scene.

It is interesting to note a psychological continuity between
the Hebrew *qahal* and Dr. King's audiences. The word *amen* is,
of course, Hebrew, with the meaning "yes," "so be it," "let it
stand!" Dr. King's audiences, largely Black and Southern,
reared in a world much influenced by the Old Testament, were
not simply shouting a Hebrew word. They were at least uncon-
sciously using the word in the same manner that the Hebrew
congregation did. "And the people cried, 'Amen'!" is a common refrain in the Old Testament. Its meaning is now clear.
The people said, "Yes, let it be." And the preceding became
endorsed as part of the *pleroma*.

Creative Memory Lapses

Two Harvard scholars, M. Parry and A. B. Lord, have accomplished much in researching a more formal type of oral composition that continues to live in our own age. Until fairly recently a type of Yugoslavian poetry was transmitted only orally. With the use of wire and tape recorders, Parry and Lord carried on a study of this transmission over a period of some decades. Their observations make possible some conjectures on the mode of oral transmission in the Old Testament.

The amazing power of the memories of the people who transmitted the poetry was largely substantiated. However, there were exceptions. Most interesting was the observation that the occasional memory lapses were not noted by the performing poets themselves. One of them had told the researchers, "If you come back in twenty years, I shall repeat this without changing a word." An easy boast, one might say. In fact, one of the researchers did return in seventeen years, recorded and compared the two tapes. There were brief but significant changes. And the poet was totally unaware of the changes that had been made.

While other explanations can be offered, this does make one intriguing explanation possible. The instincts of a great entertainer become so sensitive to audience reaction that a modification of previous performances (technically called a *shtick* by modern Jewish performers) can be made without conscious awareness. When that performance is limited to oral recitation, subtle changes in the composition are so made. The performer may not be consciously aware of the subtle changes, but they are substantially influenced by audience reaction. Thus is the *pleroma* attained.

JEDP

Among those who hold for the existence of "sources" in the Old Testament, whether oral or written, there is consensus on the existence of four special sources labeled *J*, *E*, *D* and *P*. These sources are so named because the *J* source uses the name *Jahweh* for the Divinity, while the *E* source calls Him *Elohim*. The *D* source is largely found in the book of Deuteronomy and is "humanistic," while the *P* source is "priestly." It represents the Hebrew religion of a certain genre. It is preoccupied with a certain kind of religious practice, with precision in cult and fidelity to rubrical detail. Even this brief description of the four sources shows the reasonableness of suspecting that these theologies were once separated. (The Appendix to this book offers a chart showing how much of the Pentateuch is broken down according to these sources.)

There are some practical problems in understanding the Old Testament if one does not hold for a "source" theory of some kind. For example, in Genesis 18, there is some confusion whether Abraham's visitor(s) is singular or plural. A plural verb is sometimes used for the visitor(s); another time a singular verb is used. Noah's sacrifice in Genesis 8 is compatible with Genesis 7 but not with Genesis 6. (Chapter 6 admits to the ark only a single pair of animals of each species, and the later sacrifice would wipe out the species. Genesis 7, however, admits seven pairs of such animals to the ark.)

However, it is not precisely such practical problems that make the source-theory necessary and attractive. It is the serious differences in theological dimensions that make the theory worthwhile. Each of the sources differs gravely from the other in major points of very basic theology. In some ways, for example, the *Jahwist* sees the Divinity in a more "primitive" manner than do the other sources. "Primitive" is not altogether a pejorative word. The *Jahwist's* description of the Divinity admits of a greater affectivity; he describes the Divinity in rather human language. It is fairly clear that the *Jahwist* is aware of the limitations of that language, but he uses it because it is redolent of a warmth and tenderness that more precise theological language cannot express. God walks in the garden "in the cool of the day" (*Gen.* 3:8). The figure here is that of any reasonable person living in the ancient Near East. He takes an afternoon nap in the heat of the day, rises for a refreshing drink and takes advantage then of the cool, later afternoon breeze before settling down for another period of work in the cool evening. This Divinity seems to learn gropingly. He notices that Adam is not happy living by himself, so he creates many other animals. Apparently realizing that Adam is still not satisfied, he moves on to the creation of woman (*Gen.* 2:18-

22). The creation of woman takes place in a human (but magical) fashion. The *Jahwist* God personally takes a rib from the side of Adam (after causing a deep, pain-killing sleep to fall on him) and "shapes" it into a woman. Then he thoughtfully fills up the hollow spot in Adam with flesh. After Adam and Eve sin, this Divinity himself makes garments for them out of skin (*Gen.* 3:21). The *Jahwist* Divinity, then, is a warm and tender person. He apparently has limits, however, to his power, and worries about losing it. He puts man out of the garden because man is getting too close to his divine immortality (*Gen.* 3:23). He hears reports about tower-building on the part of men (*Gen.* 11) and "comes down" from heaven to take a look for himself. He grows concerned and fears once again that man will take some of his power, so he has to take stern measures.

The *Jahwist* Divinity has, then, a realistic view of men. He is concerned with his own power, but fearful that men would make bad use of it if they got control of similar power. The *Jahwist* theologian sees this Divinity as the God of Israel. He sees that the Hebrew people are specially obligated to him and that these obligations must be fulfilled in certain limited ways. The *Jahwist* Ten Commandments are "ceremonial" or "rubrical" (*Ex.* 34). What is it to be a pious believer? One must observe precise rituals. The *Jahwist* Ten Commandments make no mention of any obligation to one's neighbor. From the viewpoint of a later and more sophisticated theology, this is perhaps the "weakness" of the *Jahwist* theology. It implies the possibility that the *Jahwist* Divinity can be "controlled" somehow by men and that to appease him, one need only observe certain rituals.

The *Elohist* Divinity is the mighty Lord of History. There is little anthropomorphism in any description of him. He is the God of the entire world; he is not simply the God of Israel, although he has a special love for her. Most precisely, he is the God who cannot be frustrated. Joseph's brothers meant to do him harm; in fact, their wills were evil. Nonetheless, the Lord that rules history used even their evil intent to draw forth good for Joseph and the nation (*Gen.* 50). Abimelech may not have been well-intentioned in the matter of Abraham's wife. Still, he did not approach her sexually because the *Elohist* Divinity would not permit him to err in this matter (*Gen.* 20). Even though Abimelech seemed unconscious of the divine power, still that power kept him from evil. The *Elohist* Ten Commandments answer the question, "How is the Divinity to be pleased?" with some reference to one's obligation to the neighbor whose life, spouse, property and reputation are to be heeded (*Ex.* 20).

The other major sources may be summarized even more briefly. The *D* source is "humanistic," but in no sense that is opposed to religious thought. Rather, it is humanistic in the sense that a previous generation of Christian theologians spoke of an "incarnational humanism." For *D*, the Divinity's work lies very much on earth. The purpose of the law is to enable men to spread the extent of that law to other men and to make its effects felt. For example, if *D* will tolerate slavery, the slave nonetheless has rights (*Deut.* 15:12-18). He is a "brother" and the Hebrew is reminded that he himself was once "a slave in Egypt."

The *P* source has values of its own. The *P* creation account (*Gen.* 1:1-2:4a) is possessed of a stately dignity. The Lord sees how good creation is. He too is a tender God. To the ancient Hebrews who might have feared sun, moon and stars as hostile divinities, he offers a reminder that they are only "lamps!" (*Gen.* 1:14 *me'oroth*). And if this Divinity is to be worshipped with rubrical precision, the precision is not mechanical. It is simply a kind of precision that is seemly for a God that is quite dignified.

The consensus of scholars who see these as discrete sources dates them within the following broad framework: *J* comes from a period around 950 B.C., *E* circa 850, *D* circa 622, and *P* after the Exile (550). With all that has already been said about complexity of composition, transmission, and "schools" of authorship, these dates should be interpreted only as general frames of reference.

Developments from This Theory

Even scholars who are convinced that the above theory is

truly insightful are not totally happy with the way the theory grew in Old Testament scholarship. One generation of scholars after another worked on the theory. Each attempted to build on the work of the scholarly generation that preceded. This led to a sort of contest in which one scholar tried to outdo another in finding, ingeniously, a greater and greater complexity in the matter of sources. The naming of sources grew steadily more complicated, one new stratum after another was "discovered," until a necessary reaction had to set in. Today, all but the most unbridled of enthusiasts for the *JEDP* theory would agree that a *reductio ad absurdum* was beginning to overtake a very good thing. And some retrenchment has begun.

What are the precise advantages of the theory? Many people feel the theory helps explain some "inconsistencies" in the Old Testament. Still, there may be far more to the *JEDP* theory than that. It is among the firmest dicta of the Judaeo-Christian tradition that the Divinity is immense, enormously beyond the capability of man to grasp. To some of us, *JEDP* is an echo of this feeling. Hopefully, even the brief sketch offered of *J*, *E*, *D* and *P* has shown them to be deeply divergent theologies. If this is so, then each of them could be offering a flash of insight into an infinite Divinity whom man cannot possibly understand with any degree of perfection. The tenderness of that Divinity as seen in *J*, the immensity proclaimed by *E* are aspects of one and the same Divinity. In attempting to answer the question, "How is such a Divinity to be approached?", *J*, and *E*, and *D*, and *P* answer with proclamations of ceremonial decalogue, one that is at least partially ethical, one that insists on a valid "humanism," and one that puts stress on rubrical precision. But each of them is implicitly saying the same thing (while saying many other things). In chorus, the sources teach that the Divinity of the Old Testament can be described by men only in a most limited fashion. This is so, of course, because man is limited. Basically, however, it is so because the Divinity of the Old Testament most emphatically is *not* limited.

There may well be competent Old Testament scholars about today who are not satisfied with *JEDP* on academic grounds, and there is no need to quarrel with them. It is more difficult to be patient with those who dispute *JEDP* on religious grounds and who are apprehensive about the notion of the coexistence in the Old Testament of theologies that differ among themselves. Perhaps these apprehensions may be assuaged by the realization that the differences among *JEDP* are surely less than those which the ecumenical movement is discovering among various religious groups. And even those differences are quite tolerable if one views them thus: "If theology teaches us anything, it teaches us that the Divinity is greater than any one of us and greater than any group of us. Religious men are basically ignorant folk kneeling in the dust at the foot of Mount Sinai and seeing the Divinity only in flashes of lightning followed by long periods of darkness. Religious men who have any wisdom at all use the periods of darkness to turn to their neighbor and ask: 'tell me, what did you see that my vision may be full!' "

This theory does nothing but illustrate the greatness of the One of Sinai, whose reality is seen, now by one source, now by another, only in flashes of brief illumination, so that only by putting all these fragmented insights together can we assemble a vision which remotely touches the greatness of the One who is.

4

The Aforesaid
Proven by Examples

Many of us have vivid memories of freshman college English. The initial mystery, at least as approached in Jesuit colleges, was the subtle distinction between the "difficult" and the "obscure" in the writing of poetry. Eventually the distinction dawned on even the slower student. If the professor could understand the poem, it was merely difficult; otherwise it was obscure. Some are reminded of this mild cynicism when they begin to read Old Testament source analyses. The experts differ among themselves. Over a long enough academic lifetime a given expert may contradict himself. For this reason, it might have been the part of prudence to avoid any such direct analysis in this book. However, sufficient prudence in the writing of a book can lead to extreme boredom. And that is to be avoided.

In the course of this brief chapter, some discussion will be offered of various sources that appear in parts of Genesis. En route, we shall also do other things.

The Judaeo-Christian Tradition

The expression "Judaeo-Christian tradition" has already been used more than once in the book and will recur. Perhaps a definition is necessary. Some persons, notably those most sympathetic to Jewish theology as a growing thing, do not care for the phrase. They feel it is inextricably bound to a number of Christian prejudices. One of these presupposes that Christianity is a living result from a dead predecessor—the world of

Hebrew-Jewish thought. An analogous prejudice sees a value in the Hebrew pattern, but views the end of the Old Testament period as marking *finis* to Hebrew thought. For persons of this prejudice, Christianity is alive and vital, while the Old Testament world died irrevocably with the final destruction of the Temple. The founding of modern Israel is only a slight embarrassment to this position. This latter prejudice also sees Christian thought as one continuous, healthy dynamic of growth, from the experience of the resurrection to the present. There is, in fact, an interesting parallel between the adjustments which Christianity had to make when the *parousia* did not immediately come and those which Israel had to make with the final destruction of the Temple. But the parallel is lost on many Christians.

Furthermore, some Christians when they use the expression "Judaeo-Christian" imply that all reflective theological development in Israel ceased with the close of the Old Testament period and was succeeded by the vigor of the New Testament world which lasts with us to the present time.

The above prejudices, of course, are unfounded in fact. The close of the Old Testament period simply marked the end of an epoch in the history of the Hebrew people. From that day until this, Hebrew thought has continued to flourish in the theological sphere. Like all theological continua, the Hebrew-Jewish world has had epochs that were more exciting or fruitful (not necessarily the same) than others. But it has continued to grow theologically.

When the expression "Judaeo-Christian" is used in this book, then, it means simply that there are values in the two worlds of Hebrew-Judaism and of Christianity that are common. It is certainly true that early Christianity derived most of its basic values from a second-century B.C. Judaism that was far more complex than has been realized until recently. This was the continuation of the phenomenon by which the Hebrew world derived many of its basic values, as we shall subsequently see, from the world around it. Even theologically we learn from our neighbors. The common values of Judaeo-Christianity are many. They become eminently visible if compared even cursorily with those religions which stand outside the Judaeo-Christian stream. In fine, then, the expression Judaeo-Christianity, even though it can have poor connotations, can also bear a freight of commonality and ecumenism. So is it used in this book.

Old Testament Theology

There are at least two valid methodologies of Old Testament theology. The first occupies itself with an effort to show the state of theological reflection in a given era and touching on a particular point. It can ask a question such as, "What was the definition of 'the Just Man' in the patriarchal period or in the period of the Judges?" This methodology, of course, must define its terms very carefully. When one says, "period of the Judges," is the actual heroic age of Israel meant, or does the speaker refer to the period, some centuries later, when the book of Judges was compiled? In the latter case, the scholar must carefully sort out, to the extent that this is possible, any value judgments which are truly those of the writers of the Book of Judges, and judgments which those writers faithfully transmitted, believing them to be the judgments of the ancient heroic period. A student of this methodology clearly must concern himself with careful analysis of sources.

There is another valid methodology. This one attempts to study the Old Testament from a somewhat timeless viewpoint and to appraise the position offered by the entire Old Testament on a given topic. To a certain extent, students of this methodology must concern themselves with the vantage point of the final redactor. This is possible with some degree of accuracy, of course, only in those areas where the theological viewpoint of the final redactor himself can be clearly determined.

To some extent, both of these methodologies will influence the development of this chapter.

The Old Testament and Loyalty

Many clergymen in this decade have had the following experience. A person who is married (or in the Roman church bound by life-long vows to a Religious Order) decides to break off the relationship. The clergyman who is counsellor in the process finds himself listening to a lengthy paragraph, pointing out that no lifelong commitment is possible, that personalities change from day to day, that it is naive psychology to say that the person I am today can be bound by commitments I made a decade ago, in another world, when I was another person.

Certainly, lifelong commitment to a relationship between persons has never been an easy thing. Such relationships are dynamic. Each half of the relationship often changes significantly in a lifetime. And, of course, there are experiences where a variety of complicated causes may make a rupture justifiable, even ethically commendable.

Still, even if the above reflective description of a life-situation were translatable into Old Testament terms, the pious citizen of the Old Testament world would find much in this line of reasoning unacceptable. For if one is looking for a single term to describe the Old Testament's view of the mutuality that governs the relationship between the Divinity and man, or the relationship between those persons who are bound together in a common love of that Divinity, the single term could well be loyalty or loyal commitment.

And there is a special dimension of that loyal commitment that should be cited. It is important in itself. Moreover, it helps us to understand how something more precise than "treaty-language," namely, "covenant-language," came to play such an important role in the Old Testament. In the covenant formulary, there was a paragraph of *stipulations*, the requirements that the lesser person or power took on himself to show his fidelity to the great lord. It was often stressed that the suzerain did not need anything that the lesser powers had to offer. For the suzerainty treaties around Israel, of course, this was largely literary license. Obviously the suzerain stood to gain something from the covenant or he would not have entered into it. Still, the Hebrew religious leaders saw this form as perhaps even more suited to their purposes than to its original use; they seized on it, perhaps precisely because of the insistence that the lord, in this case the Divinity of Israel, did not need anything from his subjects.

Almost as a corollary of the above, one of the stipulations frequently occurring in such treaties was that the participants should show love and fidelity to all other participants in the treaty—to their equals who were in a similar relationship to the great power. This is so, of course, since the Divinity does not need anything. Faithfulness to him is shown by manifesting a loving graciousness to one's fellow vassals who are in need of that graciousness. Further treatment of the stipulations can be left to a later chapter.

Loyal Commitment Often Renewed

It is this deep concern with loyal commitment that makes three chapters of Genesis (12, 15, 17) so interesting. The chapters are redolent of treaty language. They differ in emphases only. Although one Old Testament scholar cautions that the occurrence of treaty language can never be surprising. In the ancient East, the meeting of one tribe with another could be concluded only in one of two ways: by a battle or a treaty; silent passage was unthinkable. This being the case, we cannot be surprised by the prevalence of treaty language in Old Testament expression. The emphases show us hints of lifestyles in the ancient world that are centuries apart from one another.

Nor is this treaty-language limited to relationships with the Divinity of Israel. The prophet upbraids the people who do not fear the approaching wrath because they say, "We have made a treaty with Mot, a pact with Sheol" (*Is.* 28:15). The language here is that of Hebrew religion and its antecedents. The major difference, of course, is the clear expression of an idea that mainstream Hebrew theology largely abandoned for its view of the Divinity—that he can be controlled. The prophet scorns persons who feel that their agreement with the powers of darkness will defend them against just punishment. Their ideas are a throwback to an idea which Israel had quite rejected.

Covenants—Conditioned and Unconditioned

In some writing on the notion of Covenant (including material which appears in my book *The Threshing Floor*), a distinction is introduced whose significance is perhaps exaggerated. Some authors write that some covenants between God and Man in the Hebrew Bible are *conditioned* and some are *unconditioned.* The prime example of the former is the Mosaic covenant, and of the latter the Davidic. The difference between the two, it is said, is this: One requires fidelity to commandments as a necessary condition for the continuation of the covenantal relationship, and the other does not. This is probably an oversimplification. It is true that the Davidic covenant gives a specific assurance that violations on the part of man will not destroy the relationship (*2 Sam.* 7:14-15); nonetheless, it is clearly implied that man ought not to indulge in such violations. As for the guarantee of God's forgiveness, there are guarantees and guarantees. One may state it in words or demonstrate it through example. In one source which follows on the revelation of the Sinai covenant, a monstrous violation of the covenant follows almost immediately: the worship of the golden calf. The Divinity is properly enraged and threatens total punishment of the nation. Moses prays (*Ex.* 32:32) "May you forgive this people of yours . . . Or blot me out of your book!" There is no blotting done. We are told (verse 34) that the people will eventually be punished and that they were punished (verse 35). The punishment, though, must have lacked spectacular drama (if it took place), or it would have been recorded. Moreover, the passage cited in 2 Samuel (as an example of the Davidic covenant) promised punishment for violations, but it also promised that violations would not lead to rupture. This is precisely the case here with the Mosaic covenant. So what is the difference between the two presentations?

One difference is this: The quality of mercy in the Exodus

account is attributed not to the Divinity, but to Moses who "stands up to God." The passage can be read in such fashion as to conclude that Moses somehow or another "restrained" the Divinity. This is most interesting. To a more precisely theological mind than the one which proposed the idea cited in verse 32, this is impossible. No one restrains the Divinity. It may be difficulty with this notion that caused another hand to suggest in later verses that it did not work, that the people got punished anyway. Even if this were the case, the Divinity is still "restrained." The implied threat for such violations is not punishment, but annihilation. And it does not take place.

There is an interesting parallel in Roman Catholicism to the theologizing that is done in these verses. The uneducated Catholic, at least of a few years ago, sometimes tended to see the Virgin Mary as "restraining" the Divinity, as being somehow a force outside him. The theologian, on the other hand, saw the Virgin as a creature of the Divinity, whom he used to evoke his mercy, even at the risk of seeming "restrained" by her. It was this general view of the Virgin which became famous, for different audiences, in Cardinal Newman's paragraph from *The Glories of Mary* and then again in *The Portrait of the Artist as a Young Man* where James Joyce used it:

> He once had meant to come on earth in heavenly glory but we sinned; and then He could not safely visit us but with a shrouded majesty and a bedimmed radiance for He was God. So . . . He sent Thee, a creature in his stead, with a creature's comeliness and lustre suited to our state. And now thy very face and form, dear mother, speak to us of the Eternal; not like earthly beauty, dangerous to look upon, but . . . telling of heaven and infusing peace.

However the dynamic is to be explained, there seems to be some reluctance in men to attribute mercy to the Divinity. They wish to place that quality elsewhere, whether they do so with theological precision (seeing the "restraining" influence as a creature), or whether they view the influence as an independent force or even a lesser deity.

But even when the attribution of the divine mercy or gentleness to a creature is done with some theological precision as in the Newman/Joyce passage, it is not difficult to see how easily such a "creature" could glide into the role of lesser deity (at least for the theologically less sophisticated). So could the Virgin in the passage just cited, and so could Moses, the guarantor of mercy even in the conditioned covenant. For that reason, one source tells us that when Moses was buried, the place was kept secret, and no one knows where it is to this day (*Deut.* 34:7). Obviously, this source felt, were this or that spot pointed out as even a probable site for Moses' grave, some frail Hebrews would worship there and Jahwism would be threatened.

Covenantal Themes in Genesis

In the patriarchal chapters of Genesis, many of these themes are woven through and through—promises of loyalty on the part of the Divinity, a call for a kind of reciprocity on the part of man, and the stature of the patriarchs as a guarantor of the divine mercy when men should fail. Genesis 12 opens with a blessing of Abraham in archaic Hebrew poetry. The Divinity promises to "bless those who bless" Abraham and to "curse those who belittle" him. The *Jahwist* account attempts occasionally to cite a time or place (which the more universal *Elohist* does not bother to do). Consequently, it is possible that the mention of the "Oak of Moreh" is only an afterthought to cite a particular locale. Still, it is identified as Shechem's "holy place." *Moreh* in Hebrew can mean teacher or instruction. It probably has a more nuanced meaning here, "giver of oracles," or "maker of decisions." In any event, we are here dealing with a site that long pre-dates more sophisticated Hebrew theology. A given judge sat under a tree and made decisions. Who he was and the nature of his judicial process is lost. Still, the place remains significant enough so that it marks the spot where Abraham passed.

It is easy to lose the emotional significance of trees in the Old Testament. However, when one sees the gnarled and ancient relics still standing in the Holy Land (such as the living antique at Hebron in whose shade, the Arabs think, Abraham once sat—most unlikely!), it is easier to grasp the awe of the ancients for this wonder. In a world that is hostile and unfriendly to most forms of life, this given tree has survived. And so one is moved to wonder. It is hard to imagine the depth of this awe in the ancient world for the aged tree—or person. Antibiotics and a host of other wonders have made survival into old age not quite the marvel to us that it was for the early Hebrews. Perhaps the only analogous awe we have today for age is that experienced on meeting elderly persons who have survived not only physically but emotionally and spiritually.

The Wife-Sister

The Divinity's loyalty to Abraham is narrated by one strange episode (*Gen.* 12:10-20). On entering a foreign kingdom, Abraham instructs his wife to identify herself not as his wife but as his sister. He is, the text tells us, fearful that the ruler will want the beautiful woman for himself and would kill Abraham, if need be, to get her. The murder is not necessary if Abraham is only her brother. Scholars have pointed out an interesting origin for this story. In the Babylonian world where Abraham was at home, a woman of high rank could get herself declared by a legal fiction to be a man's "sister." This enabled her to retain control over her own property. It may be, conjecture some scholars, that the entire episode is a fictional account, springing from a later author's inability to make sense of the epithet, "wife-sister" which was faithfully handed on in description of Sarah. Not having at his disposal Babylonian documents now available to most first-year graduate students of Old Testament, this author made a healthy guess. But if he guessed wrong on the literal meaning, he underlined a more important meaning. The Divinity is faithful and true; Abraham gets his wife back. The story is told of Sarah again in Genesis 20 and of Rebeccah in Genesis 26. In the latter two cases, it is made clear that the eager monarch did not touch either of the beautiful women, although they were in his power for some time. Such is the loyalty of Israel's Lord to his vassals!

Abraham the Childless

There is another example of misunderstanding and insight in the opening verses of Genesis 15. Abraham complains that no lengthy relationship with the Divinity is really possible, that Abraham is without child and that "some man of my household will be my heir." Some scholars see in the Hebrew text, which is somewhat muddled here, an allusion to another Babylonian legal fiction contemporaneous with Abraham, the practice of adoption. One could adopt another person for a variety of reasons, some of which do not correspond to adoption in our society. One of the most common was the use of adoption as a legal fiction to avoid alienation of family property. One adopted the money-lender who would then eventually be paid from one's estate. This would no longer involve alienation of patrimony, though, since the money-lender would be collecting his own as a "son of the household." If this scholarly intuition is correct, we would have, among other things, another example of the firmness with which Abraham speaks to the Lord. "What can you do for me? I have no heir except my creditor."

Most source scholars believe chapter 15 is largely the work of the *Jahwist*. They feel that there is some *Elohist* rewriting (perhaps largely indicated by the absence of time and space indicators; the *Elohist*, remember, stresses the universality of the divine message), but there are other layers of composition. The mysterious sacrifice that takes place to mark the treaty between the Divinity and Abraham, seems to span at least two epochs. At least to the scholar devoid of experience in animal husbandry, the rubrics that call for a three-year-old heifer, a three-year-old goat, and a three-year-old ram, along with a "turtledove" and "a young pigeon," seem complicated enough to belong to a later *Priestly* era. However, this account is coupled with far more ancient details. An ancient word for darkness is used: *'altah* (verse 17). This is prepared for by the use of a "modern" word for darkness in one of the earlier verses (verse 12) (*hashekah*). The antiquity of the passage is also indicated by the cutting of the animals in half and the, implied movement of Abraham between the halves of the animals. We know the meaning of this ritual from extrabiblical sources. "As these animals have been cut in half, so may I be torn asunder if ever I should violate this covenant!" (Cf. *Jer.* 34:18.) The chapter in Genesis does not tell us that Abraham so passed between the halves of the animals. This is perhaps because the chapter would then have to admit that Jahweh himself so passed, threatening himself with punishment if he failed. These details were probably in the original story, but the *Pietas dynamic* permits a later redactor to edit here.

Covenant and Circumcision

Genesis 17 is largely *Priestly* in its composition. Among other arguments, scholars feel that this chapter places a large stress on ritual circumcision as the prerequisite for entry into the covenantal relationship. Unlike many other religions, which make this a puberty rite, the Hebrews (so says this stratum) must perform it on the infant eight days after birth. This is partially out of humanitarian reasons. The infantile nervous system is quite incomplete at this stage and—largely for this reason—infant circumcision is virtually painless. But there may be other reasons. Circumcision obviously implies that for the Hebrew sexual activity is a part of the religious sphere. The world of the Old Testament is not among those religions that would try clearly to disjoin religion and sex. For the pious Hebrew, religion must permeate one's entire life—most certainly including the sexual. The obligation of infant circumcision certainly binds the parent and is a reminder—almost from the very beginning—of his obligation to bring the child up in the way of the covenant. Finally, although the world of the Old Testament does not use the words "act" and "potency," it may well be that the Old Testament sees the infant as a potentially active sexual agent. From the very beginning, the infant will be marked among those who cannot disjoin sex and faith. For the child is to be—and in one sense already is—a Hebrew.

Abraham "Restrains" the Lord

It is not long before Abraham has a chance to test the faithfulness and loyalty of the Divinity in his covenantal agreement. In Genesis 18:16-33, the Lord decides not to conceal from Abraham his intention of destroying Sodom. Abraham quickly and vigorously assumes the role of guarantor of mercy—even for those who in this case stand outside the covenant. Will the Divinity not spare the city for fifty just men? forty-five? thirty? ten? To this last the Lord agrees. Alas, the ten are not to be found and the city perishes. And so Genesis teaches, to paraphrase Augustine, that the Lord who created us without our assistance will not save us without some feeble gestures on our part.

So far we have seen that the Hebrews came to learn that the Divinity was not impersonal force, but personal, that he was himself faithful and true and demanded some kind of reciprocity. The greatest of all their insights, of course, was that "the Lord our God is one" (*Deut.* 6:4), and that we shall examine in the next chapter.

5

Our Lord Is One—
He Alone

Old Testament theologians spend a good deal of time on studying *henotheism* and *monotheism* in the Old Testament. As the terms are generally understood, the former means a limited belief in the superiority of one god. This god is certainly given preferential treatment by the faithful. Still, his faithful do not expressly deny the existence of other gods; they may believe these other gods have limited spheres of influence. They most probably judge them to be inferior to "their" god, but they neither deny their existence nor feel any guilt about the refusal to deny such existence. The monotheist, on the other hand, insists stoutly that there is only one god and that he is *God*, as normal English usage describes the difference.

First, it should be admitted that there is monotheism and monotheism. Only the precisely analytical mind of the probing theologian (hardly a majority among believers) is consistently aware of the non-divine status of evil demons or good angels. Considering the ancestry of these demons and angels, this is hardly surprising. The lesser deities of the Canaanite pantheon made an easy entrance into the Old Testament milieu and post-Old Testament writings precisely as semi-divine beings. While the Christian, quite properly, would insist that his notion of a Trinitarian Divinity in no wise conflicts with monotheism, Orthodox Judaism might see it as but one more evidence of the uneasiness with which man accepts the harsh and dreadful love of monotheism. The apocryphal pious illiterate of one Christian tradition who summed up trinitarian belief by saying, "To all intents and purposes there are three gods!" horrifies all Christians possessed of the faintest degree of theological literacy. Still, he points up one question which many non-theological religionists have to ask themselves occasionally: Monotheism—does it make a difference?

Before answering that question, one further presupposition of Old Testament scholars must be examined. Scholars of the Old Testament regularly remark that the Old Testament lacks a philosophical spirit and that the man of the Old Testament does not feel the need to reflect philosophically. The mind of Western modern man, especially the mind of the youthful Western modern man, has extreme difficulty in accepting this fact. We are so used to reflecting, confusedly and lazily at times, but with great frequency and for prolonged periods of time, that some of us tend to identify reflection (at least in the religious sphere) with commitment.

The identification, of course, is a false one. Many persons of deep religious commitment, at least in the modern West, do spend considerable portions of their time in prayerful reflection leading them frequently to pious deeds. But even in the West there are those who by temperament or education feel no need of reflection; they do not find it useful, especially in religious matters, but proceed directly to religious activity of a very high order skipping the intermediary step. For example, a long Christian tradition in the care of the sick, identifies the tedium —and worse—of the chores connected with tending the aged, dying or infirm, with service to Christ. This identification can be defended on scriptural and theological grounds. Still, one strongly suspects, the vast majority of persons engaged in such Christian service rarely reflect on the theological foundation of what they are doing. They simply do it.

This is worth stressing. The modern, the young, the Western mentality, because it esteems reflection as a constituent in its religious activity, tends to consider activity which is devoid of reflection at least faintly non-religious. This is an understandable human error. It is similar to the error of those academicians who speaking of the "quality of human life" tend to identify quality with IQ, easily reaching the conclusion then that persons with IQ's below, let us say, 50 have a very limited right to life. Prescinding from any other area of the dispute, the academician's error is this: The quality of his life has been colored by his IQ. It may be that as a child he found himself less gifted than others in physical appearance, in coordination or in the ability to give and to receive affection. In his earliest years his IQ became his Linus-blanket. In mature years, using the considerable force of that very IQ, he proceeded then to identify it with quality of human life. He has made an understandable error from his own limited experience.

This extended example has been used to highlight a simple facet of the human learning process: We must ever be on guard against our prejudices. The Western mind might see the value of monotheism through extended metaphysical reflection. But is there another way of answering the question: Monotheism—does it make a difference?

It has often been said that when one places a metaphysical question to the "man of the Old Testament," the citizen of Old Testament times whose thought processes are represented in the pages of the text, he will generally respond by saying, "Let me tell you a story!"

Sometimes the story that results may show traces of a deeply reflective mentality—manifested differently from the way we in the West are accustomed to manifest our reflection. Here for example: How does the Old Testament go about describing the significant difference of the Divinity who is introduced as *the* Divinity of the Old Testament?

In order to get some proper appreciation for the nuances of the verses which surround Exodus 3:14, one has to have some appreciation for the unique role of Moses in the Old Testament world. Moses is not simply a great charismatic figure in a library (the books of the Old Testament) which is replete with great charismatic figures. His stature is absolutely unique. Founder, prophet, guide, priest, counsellor-to-generals—Moses is incomparable. He is used to teach many lessons. Does Moses neglect circumcision (*Ex.* 4:24-26)? God almost kills him. If the great Moses could not neglect this rite, how much more you? Moses dies and is buried, and no one knows where the tomb is "to this day" (*Deut.* 34:6). Why so? If the Hebrews knew the location of the tomb, they would be inclined to worship there, partially because their grasp on monotheism is so precarious and partially because of the unique stature of Moses. Now against this background of the totally unique position of Moses in the Old Testament, how does the Exodus story treat Moses as he receives the revelation of God's most sacred name? What are the first instructions of the Divinity to this demigod among men?

"Take off your shoes. The place on which you stand is holy ground" (*Ex.* 3:5). Such is the first confrontation of the great Moses with the Divinity who is to be identified as Jahweh. Moses is instructed to approach him barefoot because even the soil to which the Divinity has become mysteriously present is by that fact so holy that even the great Moses may stand on it only when barefoot—a mark of extreme reverence in many cultures if not in our own. The Hebrew storyteller in the background is saying: "Do you want to know how great Jahweh is? Well, one day Moses tried to approach a burning bush to which Jahweh was present, and the first thing that Jahweh told him was: Take your shoes off before you even come close to my presence. That is how great Jahweh is. As great as Moses was, the dirt near to the bush to which Jahweh was present—on that dirt Moses could not stand while wearing shoes."

Earlier in the book, we noted Petrie's observation that no goldwork was to be found at Hebrew sites, that their genius was of another sort. Genius can be defined in sundry ways. If by genius we mean a kind of absolute originality, the seeing of something for the very first time, then perhaps the Hebrews would have difficulty in proving their claim to genius. But this is not the only type of genius. The second type sees the good in another's idea (even when the other does not totally see it himself).

There is strong evidence that the Hebrew genius in the area of theology was largely of this second sort. For example, the Hebrews did supply subsequent religions with the idea that God was One. But there is evidence that they absorbed this idea from religions which preceded theirs. Even the sacred name Jahweh may have come from non-Hebrew origins into the Hebrew circle.

Before proceeding further, it might be worth examining the ways in which good ideas may fail in a given society if the society is not ready for them or if the ideas are not properly presented. American historians note that Adlai Stevenson II called for the abolition of the draft and a nuclear test ban treaty in the dying days of the 1956 presidential campaign. He was widely pilloried in the press. He was accused of "clutching at straws" in a campaign that was going nowhere. He of course lost the election and eventually died—but the ideas lived. Nearly two decades after he had proposed them, the ideas were officially adopted. A good idea is just about useless—until it is somehow "sold."

So it was with the notion of monotheism under the form of "Aten-Worship" in Egypt. This form of worship, as nearly as can be determined by students of Egyptian history, had its origins in the work of a small minority of theological scholars. These scholars were distressed by the simplistic polytheism of the Egyptian religion of their time. Through serious study and great metaphysical insight, they concluded to the superiority of a single god—whom they hailed as Aten, the sun-disk. With this new theological insight, they proceeded then to revolutionize Egypt. What they neglected to notice was that a religion which intellectuals found to be hopelessly simplistic, the body of the simple folk found to be rather pleasant and comforting. The resulting emotional upheavals which the forced introduction of the new religion caused were considerable. Under attack, that mode of religion which was not acceptable to the vast body of the populace was first modified and then abandoned utterly.

This version of monotheism, then, was quite short-lived in the long history of Egypt. According to at least one chronology, this short span of Egyptian monotheism coincided with Hebrew presence in Egypt. Could it be a coincidence? Of course the explanation from coincidence can never be eliminated, but the name of the great lawgiver and interpreter of monotheism to the Hebrews, "Moses," itself admits of an Egyptian origin. Although the Hebrew Bible explains the name in terms of a folk etymology (*Ex.* 2:10), indicating that the Egyptian origins of the name (and the attendant monotheism) had long since been forgotten, the name is most likely derived from the Egyptian, *mes*, meaning "child." Since variants on this name in forms combined with the names of divinities abound in Egyptian (Raamses, Thutmosis), it is not far-fetched to suggest that the Hebrew name Moses is of similar origin. The divine component in the names we have cited was child of *Ra* or child of *Thoth*. In the name of Moses, most likely there had also been a divine component. Since the name of that deity was not JHWH, very early in the redaction process, the name was dropped out. This contributed to the non-intelligibility of the name (which remained simply "child") and facilitated the development and the acceptance of the Hebrew "folk-etymology" for the name.

Old Testament scholars are generally convinced of the presence of the Hebrews in Egypt during the period of Aten-Worship. Egyptian texts contain references, for example, to the *Hbr* people. While these references are not clearly and unmistakably describing what came to be the Hebrew nation, they do point in that direction. Again it must be noted that the fact that these references occurred at all is remarkable. In light of later history, the *Hbr* people were significant. At the time, they were only one more bothersome episode in the long and distinguished history of a mighty empire.

Analogously one could not argue to the non-presence of Golda Meir in Milwaukee in 1915 from the fact that her name did not appear in the Milwaukee newspapers at that time. Prime Minister though she may have later become, there was no significant reason to expect her name to appear in Milwaukee newspapers while she was a child. (In fact her name did appear once; she won a spelling contest!) Similarly, some phonetic difficulties with the word *Hbr* and its parallels to what came to be the word for Hebrews are not enough to dislodge the significance of the references that we do find.

The Kenite Hypothesis

Another theory on the mode in which monotheism came into the Hebrew mainstream is founded on the Hebrew contact with the Kenites—a clan of the Midianites. There is much that is attractive to this theory. The Midianites were much engaged in mining and in forging metals. Their quest of metals brought them into the Sinai area—again at an interesting point in Hebrew history. Moses has a father-in-law named Jethro, a Midianite priest (*Ex.* 3:1). In the key biblical chapter for this thesis, Exodus 18, the name JHWH is found on the lips of Jethro (verse 10), and he offers sacrifice to God (verse 12) knowing now that JHWH is "greater than other gods" (verse 11). Credence is lent to the view that Jethro here instructs Moses, rather than vice versa, by an incident which fills up the rest of the chapter. Moses receives rather explicit counselling from Jethro on his mode of governing the tribes of Israel (verses 15-26). He is told that it is not wise for him to judge all cases himself, that he would be wise to share his authority with other persons in Israel and reserve only the most difficult cases to himself. And Moses yields. It is not normal procedure in the ancient Near East for the head of a clan to meekly receive advice on how to exercise his headship. From this, some scholars conclude that Jethro had already shown himself to have a unique role in Moses' life; he had introduced him to JHWH. By this introduction, Jethro gained a powerful influence over Moses and continued to exercise it.

It sometimes seems to a reader that Old Testament scholars can make too much of "vestigial" evidence, that a mere trace of something like "Kenite influence" in the development of the Old Testament monotheism is enough to send scholars off and running. Mayhap. But it should be remembered that we have no Kenite source at our disposal, that we are studying the Kenites only through a Hebrew source, and that that Hebrew source would have to be most reluctant to admit its major contribution to subsequent religious history was inherited. (It is worth pointing out here that Christians generally study Pharisaism only through a Christian source, the New Testament.)

Finally, in addition to the location of the Midianites in the Sinai area, there is the attractiveness of a "god of the Smithies" whose appearance with flashes of lightning would fit the motif of the God of Sinai.

There is one last distracting possibility that Jahwism antedates Moses. In two Old Testament texts (*Ex.* 6:20 and *Num.* 26:59), there is reference to *Jochebed*, a name given to a woman presented as the mother of Moses. The name is compound *Jo + chebed*. The first half of the compound is an archaic form of Jahweh. The second is a noun perhaps related to the prime divine attribute, *kabod* or "glory." In any event, there is evidence here of a Jahwism which precedes Moses.

What is to be made of all this? If Joan of Arc was not distressed at the allegation that her "voices" came from her imagination—"Of course! How else can God speak to me except through my imagination?"—there is one other mode of revelation that should not distress us. God speaks—sometimes even to his prophets—through the voices of other men.

The evidence that monotheism reached the Hebrews mediately is considerable. The "coincidental" presence of the Hebrew people in Egypt at the one moment in Egyptian history when monotheism had a brief flowering moment, the contact between the smithies of the Midianite—whose god would be most at home in flashes of lightning—and the listening Moses, the tantalizing reference to *Jo* in the maternal line of Moses— it is difficult to dismiss all of these in the quest for the historical Hebrew monotheism. But why should we dismiss them?

There are, as we have said, varieties of genius. The genius of the Hebrews was not precisely an original and creative genius so much as it was an absorptive one. Which is the wiser race— the one which produces an occasional genius with creative flashes, or the one which recognizes the creative flash when it is seen? If the latter is the wiser people, then few people have been wiser than the Hebrews who embraced an idea which frightened the body of the Egyptians and absorbed the idea whose memory alone keeps the Kenites in historical consciousness.

But there is more to the absorptive genius than its receptivity. Such genius must be selective. Monotheism was one bright moment in Egyptian history. She had many darker ones, and these the Hebrews ignored. For example, Egypt survived— unthinkable though it may seem to a later age—without written law. The law at any given moment was that which the Pharaoh thought it to be. This trait was far more characteristic of Egypt than was its monotheistic moment. Still, this the

Hebrews ignored while concentrating on the insights of Aten-Worship.

The God Who Cannot Be Bought

Since we are not ancient Hebrews but modern Westerners, we may now be permitted to indulge in some reflection on the meaning of monotheism. The above heading can serve as a subtitle for this chapter, for it points up one of the main significances of monotheism. There is a dynamic deep within any religious movement that inclines the devout to wish to *manipulate* the god. The most pious of worshippers finds himself occasionally tempted to use his divinity in some fashion or other. This is most easily done, of course, if the divinity lacks something which the worshipper has. With that something, whatever it may be, the worshipper may then bribe the deity.

If there is a plurality of divinities, they must need be imperfect as there cannot be a plurality of perfections. A perfect being would have to be unique. He would also have to be unchanging. Change would imply the gaining of a perfection (impossible for a perfect being) or the losing of one (equally impossible). Such a deity is truly the deity who cannot be bribed. Humanity has nothing to offer him. The starkness of this theological fact is too difficult for most of us to live with most of the time. In the marrow of our psyches, most of us find some residue of the magical, the idea that the pious believer may somehow or another "control" the divinity. But that idea is flatly contradictory to the mainstream of Old Testament thought. How contradictory it may be would be clearly shown by the meaning of the name JHWH itself, in the sober judgment of one great Old Testament scholar of our times, "I am He Who Causes to be all the things that are," i.e., I need nothing.

The Decalogue

It is difficult to remove the decalogue from consideration against the backdrop of monotheism and the God Who Cannot Be Bought. The divinity is urged often in the Psalms not to "hide his face" from the pious worshipper (*Ps.* 13:1, 27:9, 30:7, *et alibi*). The Hebrew of many of these passages makes it clear that the "hiding" is done by the physical action of "turning." The expression is quite concrete. It alludes to a religion in which the idol is turned face to the wall as a sign of displeasure with the worshipper. When the latter is forgiven, the priest has but to turn the face back, and things are once again as they were.

With the decalogue, we are in a totally different religious world from that described in the last sentence. The "ethical decalogues" of Exodus 20 and Deuteronomy 5 present us with mysteries beyond solving. There is little doubt that they are the distillations of a long procedure of evolving ethical law. Could it be otherwise? Is it conceivable that an historical people on a single day found themselves henceforth forbidden to indulge in rape, plunder—and even thoughts thereof—and that they cheerfully acquiesced? No. Such growth had to happen over a long period of time. But even then, there was a moment of before and after. There was a period when the stern demands of the decalogue were not made—and then a moment when they were made and were heeded. What is the motivation for such a drastic change in lifestyle?

In talking of motivation for obedience to the decalogue, some scholars have had recourse to the expressions *apodictic law* and *case-law.* The latter is a little closer to the ordinary human experience. It represents an equation, "If a man shall do such and such knowingly, then shall he receive such and such as a punishment." The equation is easy to see. Its usefulness to society is not difficult to grasp. Societies cannot survive where the owners of oxen that gore are not punished for being careless about their oxen. But this is not the law-mode of the decalogue.

The decalogue is one of *apodictic law.* It states flatly: Thou Shalt! or Thou Shalt Not! There is no effort made to offer an equation, to show a sweet reasonableness in doing what is commanded. If there is any motivation offered at all, it is the stern sentence underlying all the individual commandments of the decalogue: I am the Lord!

And it is unchallenged.

There is surely a connection between the acceptance of the decalogue and the "faith-experience" of the people of Israel. One cannot, in fact, dismiss out of hand the explanation that the Old Testament itself offers, that the Divinity Himself appeared with such awesomeness that a frightened people acquiesced in taking to themselves both a divinity and a stern religious code.

For those of us who experience the Divinity as moving more mediately through history, there is another—nonetheless "religious"—explanation. The Lord of History leads his people now to a "chance meeting" with the Kenites, now to a "chance contact" with the Egyptian empire in its moment of monotheism. He brings Israel through such a variety of experiences that they desire to respond as love to love. But they are handicapped. They have come to know him as the God that does not need. And so they can offer him nothing. But as he has touched them mediately, so can they touch him mediately. If he needs nothing, his children are ever in need. In treating those other children properly, the people of Israel will reach him. So seen, the decalogue is but the amplification of an introit psalm: "Lord, Who shall dwell in your tent? Who will approach your holy mountain? The Man who walks in justice and does what is right and speaks the truth. Who does only good to his neighbor and speaks no evil about him" (*Ps.* 15:1-3).

Whether this psalm is a reflection on the decalogue, or whether some ancient source of the psalm provided the wellspring from which the decalogue flowed can be left to other scholars. What is clear is that the Old Testament—in its sternest strata—knew that God needs nothing. That to be gracious to him, we must be gracious to his other children. From this insight grew Matthew's amplification of what it meant to please God by dealing benignly with his least brethren (*Mt.* 25:40). We shall return to the decalogue for fuller treatment in a later chapter. Perhaps though if the above is understood, the heart and meaning of the decalogue is understood—and the rest is commentary.

6
Deuteronomy

In many ways, Deuteronomy is a portrait in microcosm of the major Old Testament dynamic. One can with fair ease lift out various "layers" of the work and find diverse theologies in opposition to each other, if not in contradiction. The work is all the more charming as the end product. Deuteronomy as we have it, is written in clear Hebrew prose that has made it a favorite alike with the students of beginning Hebrew and with their teachers. Its inner core presupposes contact with a *qahal* that was capable of a lofty spirituality.

Its final form presents a style that is basically homiletic and not legal. The former word is often used to describe the work of the skilled pastoral orator. He is surely interested in law and in laws. But this is not precisely his fundamental interest. He is interested rather in the keeping of laws by his flock. So his style is aimed not merely at showing the requirements of a given law, but in persuading his listeners to observe those laws. His lecturing is basically hortatory.

There is also a homiletic view of history flowing from this same desire. The homiletic historian will not deliberately falsify, but he will pass over certain complexities of historical issues. He uses history to motivate his listeners to accept certain positions or attitudes. The preacher is teacher in these circumstances. He cannot run the risk that an otherwise interested audience might be distracted by a complex digression. So he contents himself by sticking to the main point. The style of Deuteronomy is the sermon style of a college professor who preaches on Sundays. The hidden depths of historical complexities are there, but one must look for them. The surface level of the material is relatively simple, direct, and hortatory. To listen to it long enough is to be moved to act and to accept a manner of action.

The origins of the book in its various layers are open to some dispute. 2 Kings 23 offers clues to one possible explanation. This chapter lists ten vices which the good and proper king will stamp out in his realm. One can make a case that these vices are all catalogued in the book of Deuteronomy. This chapter would then support "royal origin" in a reform period. Moreover, a preceding chapter (*2 Kings* 22:8ff.) mentions that in the process of rebuilding the temple, workmen stumbled on a "book of the law." This book was eventually presented to King Josiah and became the foundation of his reform. We need not be distracted here by the objection that a reform seems to have been in process before the book was found (the temple was being rebuilt) and therefore that this book could not simply have been the basis of his reform. The simplest explanation is that a reform was indeed underway—quite possibly stemming from the bureaucracy of an earlier king. The scroll simply gave a new impetus to the procedure.

Deuteronomy and Suffering

As more than one of the later chapters in our book will show, much of the Old Testament is preoccupied with the human problem of suffering. So here. There is little doubt that much of this book was written and re-written in the years from 721 to 586 B.C. In those years, the people of Israel suffered as they were never to suffer again perhaps until our own lifetime. Their theological leaders were compelled—as such leaders are always compelled—to make some effort to find a degree of intelligibility in their suffering. Their leaders had mixed success. Some modern commentators on the Old Testament would find in the book of Deuteronomy—among other layers—a distinction between the "Ur-Deuteronomist" and the "Deuteronomic Historian." The former is the "primitive author" of Deuteronomy, and the latter is the author who believed himself to be deriving a theology from the former. This second author then composed much of the historical books that follow Deuteronomy in the English version of the Old Testament. These histories (Joshua, Judges, 1-2 Samuel, 1-2 Kings) are written from a very limited viewpoint. God rewards good and punishes evil—in this life and directly.

This view of history is quite bluntly presented. There are stereotyped summaries of each king offered. Most interesting is the recurring line, "Now the rest of the acts of King so-and-so are they not written in the Chronicles of the Kings?" In other words, if you are interested in an overview, go look it up! This historian is concerned with a limited viewpoint: Why do men suffer in our nation? And the answer is: When they (or notably their kings) follow God's law, the land prospers; when kings are disobedient, the land is chastised.

Theme of the Ur-Deuteronomist

The view just described represents a rather simplist theology. It runs the risk of going counter to the "God Who Cannot Be Bought," which we presented as one of the high points of Hebrew theology. It is a short step from accepting prosperity as something that flows from obedience to seeing obedience as the necessary cause of that prosperity.

Some scholars see the Ur-Deuteronomist as teaching something different from this. He is concerned with the immense distance that separates God from man. Even in the rewritten work, the original flashes forth: Not by bread alone does man live, but by every word that comes from the mouth of God (*Deut.* 8:3). The awesomeness of that line is easily lost on modern readers. Remember that the line was addressed to an audience which saw each annual grain crop and its resulting bread as a miracle that kept death at a distance for another year. Still, the audience is told that this is not sufficient in itself for life; real life still depends, somehow, on those words which come from God's mouth.

A Theology of Place

Another illustration for the "distant God" of the Ur-Deuteronomist is in the theology of place, such as we can find in the expression, "the place which the Lord will show you." This expression, or a variation on it, shows up more than a dozen times in Deuteronomy. It places equal stress on the fact that worship is to be centralized in a given locale and a general avoïdance of stating where that locale is. In fact, of course, through much of Israel's history, the place was Jerusalem. Still, a certain timelessness is given to the theology of place by avoiding the use of the place-name. Rather, the book stresses that there is a place, that there is a special value to worship offered in that place, and that Hebrews are to esteem this place over all others as a locus from which the God of Heaven can be most easily reached. (Nor, in later writing, is this knowledge limited to Hebrews. 1 Kings 8:41-2 tells us that foreigners will come to know of the place—now identified with the Temple— and will direct their prayers toward it as a way of reaching God.)

We tend to identify the "theology of place" with the Ur-Deuteronomist. The theology of place makes demands on man, not on God. God chooses the site. Man must come out of himself in order to pray there. A certain amount of pilgrimage is necessarily involved in any kind of serious prayer—which can only be offered at the place. To the extent that man can add anything, the theology of place says that the locale is sanctified by generations of worshipers, and becomes somehow more suited for prayer and communion with the Divinity who has re-sanctified the place by becoming again and again present to man in this site and not in others. Over the long, long history of the Hebrew language, the very word for place (*maqom*) became a synonym for God himself.

A Deuteronomic View of the Hebrew

"You have been rebellious to the Lord since the day that he

(I) knew you" (*Deut.* 9:24). With this verse, we come on one of the unusual aspects of Hebrew religious literature manifested in many layers of Deuteronomy. It makes little effort to portray the Hebrew people as a group that is in any way deserving of praise. Rather it goes to another extreme. One of the adjectives used most often to describe the people in the Hebrew Bible (although not so used in the *D* sources) is "stiff-necked" (*qešeh 'oreph*). So used are the words, "stubborn" and "rebellious." One hesitates always to say that any particular single phrase can support a theory. Still, this one expression points up the uniqueness of the historicality of the Hebrew Bible. It is a wondrous bit of nostalgia that allows any descendants to remember their pious ancestors as "stiff-necked." Other strata are surely more affected by the *pietas* dynamic than is this one. But from expressions like this a large body of American Old Testament scholars* concluded to the solid historicality of the basic Old Testament accounts.

Nonetheless, the historicality in Deuteronomy is admixed with liturgical layers. How did those layers survive? Is there not a fundamental incompatibility between vigorous historical memory and the liturgical layer? Perhaps the vigor of historical memory needs no defense. Especially in the light of these "embarrassing" recollections of Babylonian origins. (Embarrassing because they are a reminder that the Hebrews did not always live in Canaan but came from the outside, displacing prior inhabitants.)

Liturgical dynamics in Deuteronomy are very strong indeed. The historical and the liturgical continue to exist side by side (even where there might be some opposition) because of their equal strength. Readers from relatively non-liturgical religions or from a non-religious background might have some reservations on this. Contemporary Roman Catholics do not. For we

---

*Throughout this book, the validity of the so-called Albright School of OT interpretation is largely accepted. The late William Foxwell Albright and his students, much influenced by the data of archaeology, held for sturdy historicality in the earliest Old Testament accounts. The school has been challenged recently by such works as Thomas L. Thompson, *The Historicality of the Patriarchal Narratives,* and John Van Seters, *Abraham in History and Tradition,* but the academic jury is still out on these critics.

have experienced the conservatism of cult in the sturdy opposition which liturgical reform continues to meet as we write. The Eastern Church, as it prepares for a thoroughgoing reform of its own, is meeting a similar opposition precisely in the area of cult. "But the Divine Liturgy was received intact from St. John Chrysostom!" is the war cry of those resisting liturgical change in the Eastern Church. The more educated among them would be hard put to defend the veracity of the slogan. No matter. Cult is intrinsically conservative; it tends to retain the past, in language and dress, even when their meanings have been forgotten. And when the liturgical material moves from ritual to literature, the conservatism continues to assert itself.

Deuteronomy, even its present form, contains cultic vestiges that include rubrics, credal material, apodictic commandments, and *toroth*. (By this last we mean commandments of a tertiary nature—sacerdotal explanations of the force of an earlier commandment or of something derived from an earlier commandment.) Perhaps the clearest example of the above is to be found in Deuteronomy 26:4-9 which begins, "Then the priest will take the basket of first fruits from your hand . . . and you will answer. . . ." This is clearly a rubric, a description of a physical action to be performed in the course of a liturgy ("At this point the priest bows profoundly and he says"). Here the layman, as always a major figure in the Hebrew liturgy, is given a rubric. He is told of the action performed by the priest before the layman begins to recite the liturgical creed.

The creed then follows the rubric, beginning with the words: "My father was a wild Aramean. . . ." Here we are following the translation of a recent scholar who interprets the Hebrew root *'bd* in terms of an Arabic cognate. If his judgment is correct, we have even more proof for the antiquity of the credal formula. It betrays an ancient memory, not always attested to in the Hebrew Bible, that the ancestors were a wild and nomadic people. (An analogous expression, *pere'adam* shows up in Genesis 16:12 "a wild ass of a man." The earlier version probably used *pere* as an honorable epithet as it would so be used among nomadic Arabs. A later editor added *adam*, judging correctly that the later non-nomadic Hebrews might not understand the noble epithet predicated of Ishmael.)

Another possible indication of antiquity for this creed is shown by its themes. There is no mention of the Sinai event in this passage, although the creed purports to be a summary of the major truths of the religion. Rather it focuses on what some have called the Exodus motif, the wanderings of a beloved people under the protective but chastising arm of a God who would not permit them to enter "the place which he had chosen" until they were ready for it.

More Cultic Vestiges

There is a general liturgical flavor to the entire book of Deuteronomy. The solemnity of language used to date ("It was in the fortieth year, in the eleventh month, on the first day that . . ." *Deut.* 1:3) suggests a recurring festival. The constant use of cliches that suggest movement toward and from holy mountains, Seir and Horeb, are evocative of religious processions. Seir itself in the oldest poetry is considered the dwelling place of the primitive god. Some of the Hebrew verbs are used in Deuteronomy where they may well admit of non-liturgical meanings. Words like *pnh* and *sbb* have possible (non-liturgical) meanings of simply turning from one place and moving in circular fashion toward another. But there were words available to the Hebrew author which carried less liturgical freight. It is hard not to see an echo here, for example, of the liturgical procession which seems to be the first imposition of the word *sbb* (as in *Ps.* 26:6, "I shall wash my hands among the innocent and *process* about your altar, O God!").

So the Deuteronomic account of movement in the wilderness is no less historical for being liturgical. This liturgy flows from history and is intended to imitate it. As the Christian liturgy is intended to evoke a living memory of past historical events, so this evocative narrative, with its recollection of liturgical feasts, processions and offerings, is intended to bring to mind much of the historical memory which underlies Hebrew theology.

Levitical Traces

Mention has already been made of *toroth*. The word has been defined as secondary or tertiary commandments flowing from primary commandments through interpretation and study. The primary commandments are presented only through charismatic leadership. One justification for the authority of charismatic leadership is found in the words attributed to Moses in Deuteronomy 18:15ff. "God will raise up other prophets. You begged for this yourselves that you might not have to hear the voice of God."

A charismatic person could offer bold new commandments on his own. Lesser religious leaders, such as the Levites, could offer only interpretations of earlier commandments. For example, Deuteronomy 5:18 and 21 specifically object only to adultery in deed or in thought as sexual violations. Deuteronomy 27:21-23 widens the prohibition considerably, forbidding sexual intercourse with a man's widowed mother-in-law, with any animal, with his sister or half-sister. (It is interesting to note here that the people cry "Amen," leading us to believe that this was seen as new teaching and therefore in need of approval by the *qahal*.)

The antiquity of the original oral composition into which these prohibitions have been inserted is quite clear. Deuteronomy 27:12-13 consists basically in a "name-list" of the tribes divided into two portions, with Levi, as always, standing apart. Some scholars feel that the most ancient form of composition is that of simple name lists and that these lists are then brought together by the "principle of coagulation." If this is so, the chapter is an excellent example of a name list that is left undisturbed. The later name Levi is simply added in a separate place, and the whole is used as a framework for the quite new *toroth* which follow.

An objection is sometimes raised to the theory of strong Levitical influence in Deuteronomy. The objection would go something like this: One of the major themes of Deuteronomy is the role of glorious conquest, but ought priests to be involved in that? This objection comes from the backdrop of a world other than that of the ancient Near East. In the Hebrew world and outside of it, the priest was much involved in all things military. No wise ancient general would think of going to war without a faithful priest at his side. His role was not simply that of "morale officer" as in modern armies. Rather he was deeply involved in the conflict. His was the role of blessing friends and cursing enemies. He might also be called on to read the signs of the future as a skilled soothsayer. In light of this, there is no surprise that one of the major themes of Deuteronomy is a "theology of conquest." The priestly personnel was much involved in battle. He had an education which inclined him to reflect. With the end of battle, he would be compelled by an inner urgency (if not by national policy) to write down the fruits of his reflection.

The Act of Entering

It is usual to observe that cultic activities are supposed to be re-enactments of activity which is taking place in "Heaven." Activity in the sanctuary then can bring about (in religions where the god is under control) a corresponding activity in the dwelling place of the god. In the Hebrew religion, a further dimension is added to this. With the eventual building of the temple, the sacred place becomes limited, and with the construction of the holy of holies, the sanctuary was even more limited. It was not always that way. The land itself, the "holy land," is in its entirety both temple and sanctuary. In the midst of a lament for Jerusalem composed in Babylon, the psalmist gives utterance to the above theme, "How can we sing to God in a foreign land." If Jerusalem is especially holy, the land *in toto* is also holy. One may assuredly sing to God outside of Jerusalem. Outside of Palestine? Perhaps not.

Because of all this, the Deuteronomic concern with the act of entering the Holy Land is more than a mere geographic or historical description. The very act of entering the land is itself sacral. With the building of the temple, with the evolution of a more specialized priesthood, some of this notion may have been lost or rather transferred. In the later New Testament letter to the Hebrews, Christ is described as the high priest par excellence precisely because he entered once and for all the sanctuary of Heaven (*Heb.* 9:11). The entire Hebrew people had long since staked out their claim to royal priesthood by entering the sanctuary of Palestine.

Deuteronomy is the liturgical book flowing from that historical entry. Moreover, it probably contains, as we have seen, allusions to processional re-enactments of that event. To other indications already cited we may add the Deuteronomic use of the root *zpn* in Deuteronomy 2:3 and 3:27. The geography of this period is not clear. It is possible that the words can simply mean "north" as they are generally translated. But in context, it seems more likely that we have here allusions to Mount *Zpn* of the Ugaritic material (a large body of "pagan" material contemporaneous with the earliest Hebrew material we have). The Ugaritic *Zpn* was the primitive dwelling place of the god and a locus of ancient pilgrimages.

One Other View

Some scholars put a greater stress on the "royal origin" aspect we mentioned earlier. They read the book of Deuteronomy with a slightly different emphasis. They see its major concerns as *paranesis* (ethical exhortation), the law, the cult, and political and military leadership. Thence they conclude that only one source in ancient Israel could be concerned with all of these: the king himself. At least three of the above themes seem rather obvious once they are pointed out. The king is surely the political and military leader; on the major feasts, even in temple times, he and not the high priest is the principal liturgical celebrant; the most vital of all legal decisions are referred to him. Some might question the role of the king as "moral leader" in a country which had a plethora of religious figures.

There is one linguistic argument which buttresses the view that the king played a major role in the shaping of Deuteronomy. The phrase which we have cited so often, "a place which the Lord will choose," employs the Hebrew root *bhr* as a word for "choose." The word has an interesting history. Some scholars feel that the word's meaning of "choose" is a late development in Hebrew. (Cognates in more ancient languages bear other semantic freight.) They judge that the word came to have this meaning first in late monarchical times and was used first in application to the choice of a king, then with regard to the choice of the chosen people, and only third for the choice of the chosen land. If this judgment is correct, the emotional overtones of the word would be something like the following: Even as the people chose me (or my father) as their king, so the Divinity has chosen this people as his special people, and this land as his very special land.

A further argument for the connection between Deuteronomy and the king can be found in Chapter 17. This chapter concerns itself with some of the duties of the king. It warns him against accumulation of too many wives or horses, as either would cost too much (verses 16-17). And then there is a remarkable instruction on what he is to do while sitting on the throne, *yošeb 'al kiss'e.* This phrase seems to be a technical expression with a couple of meanings. The one that makes the most sense here would have to do with his installation. In that very act, he is to write out a copy of the law, in the presence of the priests and levites, to keep his handwritten copy with him all the days of his life and to read from it regularly. However, such literacy on the part of the earlier kings is unlikely. So what we have here is a recollection of a relationship between the king and his royal scholars, men chosen from the *qahal.* They were with him from the day of his installation. They read the law to him and listened as he recited the law (with modifications) back to them. Perhaps some later king did indeed read the law aloud to them (as one Hebrew variant has it). Thus in an intimate dialogue, which was but an updated version of the ancient dialogue between religious leader and *qahal,* the king and his royal scholars worked out the meaning of the old law for a new time.

Conclusions

This chapter has argued for the complex origins that still assert themselves in the book of Deuteronomy. The work of the Ur-Deuteronomist and the Deuteronomic Historian is yet visible. Earlier liturgical origins—such as a certain provenience from the amphictyonic period when Israel was but a loose confederation of tribes, the influence of the Levites and a later priesthood, the contribution of kings and royal scholars in the judgment of some—are still quite visible. What are we to make of the final redaction? Much of the entire work can be read as a single sermon. If the reader hesitates at this, he should realize that sermons of hours' length are characteristic still of many contemporary religious denominations—if not of his suburban parish church. The last redactor was surely a pastoral orator. With consummate skill he wove together the contributions of all that had preceded him. With the emotion and the concern of a pastor, he urged his flock to "choose life!"'(*Deut.* 30:15-20), seeing that correctly as the great theme that tied together the best of all that had preceded him in the writing of Deuteronomy.

He offered them the choice between life and death. He urged them to be faithful to the commandments, not for hope of reward, but because such fidelity represented the highest form of life available. Like all leaders who preach a doctrine of love, in and outside of religious spheres, he knew that love is shown by deeds rather than words. He saw the complexities of the Deuteronomic legislation as truly liberating, since it left the *qahal* free in the fullest sense to show its love for the Divinity. "Obey him and you will prosper" is the major thrust of the later redactor; even so phrased, it admits of a benign interpretation. Prosperity broadly understood in terms of health and happiness may well be something that flows intrinsically from obedience to the Divinity. It is not so much that the Divinity makes an extrinsic decision to reward good and punish evil as that the doers of good and evil truly choose life or death for themselves. Generally speaking, the doers of good choose a moderation in life style, a security in family living that provides a fortress against stress and increases the chances of prosperity as most men understand it—a long and healthy life. Doers of evil, frequently if not always, bring on themselves a variety of ills due to immoderation.

But our pastoral orator was preaching far more than a kind of Hebrew stoicism. The loftiest message of Deuteronomy, even in its present form, is that obedience to the law is good because the Divinity wills it so. This is a difficult message. Only a deeply altruistic *qahal* of high religious motivation could enable the preacher to teach such a lesson.

The Deuteronomist's message was not always understood. An obedience to law that derives from fear is burdensome; if it derives from perfect love, it is joyous.

That the hearers in front of him, and those in the future, would become gifted with perfect love is something that the Deuteronomic preacher always presumed.

Such perfect love, alas, has not always been the case.

7

Idle Servants
and Worthless

In any relationship of love, there is an element of challenge
and response. There is little question that this challenge and
response lie at the foundation of the Old Testament's ex-
change between Jahweh and the children of Israel. What is
open to question (and often questioned by scholars), is the precise manner in which the relationship was spelled out. What
acts of love presented the challenge? Exactly what were the
great acts of God done for the Hebrew people? How was the nation called into being? From what was it called? To what was it
called? And when these questions are answered, others still
remain. Notably, what was the manner in which Israel answered the challenge? One is tempted to sum up this chapter by
saying that Israel concluded that the commandments were
terribly important, but that when one had kept them all, one
had not done very much.

John's gospel (14:15) describes Jesus of Nazareth as saying, "If you love me, you will keep my commandments." In
this, the Johannine school places Christ in a long, long religious tradition. Religious leadership—acts of goodness and love
on the part of the greater figure in any relationship—calls for
some kind of response on the part of the community. Frequently that response takes the form of a behavior code or ethical
system. Over a long enough period of time, the community
comes to understand itself and the call which has been made to
it in a special way. For pedagogical reasons the self-understanding is encapsulated into a series of fairly short and easily
memorized sayings; hence, commandments.

Suppositions as to the type of community activity which gave rise to the commandments may be treated elsewhere. Some were noted in an earlier chapter. Here let it be said that a kind of catechesis underlies some of the "liturgies" which lurk in the Old Testament text as we have it. In Deuteronomy 6:20, for example, there is mention of a question being asked and the subsequent memorized response being given. It is interesting to note that in a parallel passage, Deuteronomy 26:5ff., there is a rubric of answering, but no mention of a question being asked.

"And you will answer (*'anitah*)." Translations variously wriggle around the clear meaning of "answering a question" here because no question appears in the text. Translations say "confess" or "make response." But the ordinary meaning of the word is to answer a direct question. Perhaps what happened with the text is that the question itself was edited out in early times. Is the missing question analogous to that of Deuteronomy 6:20, "Your son asks, 'what is the meaning of these laws and statutes?' " Mayhap. The answer to that puzzle would take us far afield. Here we can be content with the conviction that both of these *Deuteronomic* passages further support the conviction that challenge and response lie at the heart of Hebrew theological development.

When we earlier discussed the possibility that the Covenant model underlay the Old Testament's self-understanding, we had some problems. The nature of the covenant model or suzerainty treaty model is clear. Good evidence exists (some of it presented in *The Threshing Floor*) for a Hittite model. Other scholars have suasively argued that Semitic models contemporary to the patriarchal period may just as easily be cited. What is common to both of these models is that they describe a relationship between a lesser and a greater power. They are no mere contracts between individuals of equal rank. But in each case, the question remains: Why did the Hebrew people settle on this political model as the appropriate means of relating to the God of Israel?

No totally satisfactory answer to the question exists. There are some suggestions that can be made, however. In some of the pre-Hebraic models, one of the *stipulations* (the obligations

of the lesser person in a treaty) is this: All vassals in such treaties must live in peace among themselves; they must display
the same graciousness to one another which the great Lord in
the vassal treaty deserves for himself. This stipulation supposes that the great power in the treaty really needs nothing for
himself; affection and loyalty toward him can thus be shown
only by showing it to the ordinary folk who have the same relationship to him as the one showing affection. For the Hittite
and other treaty models, this was a literary fiction. Their great
lords derived benefit from the treaty, or they would not be in it.
But the Hebrew people may well have felt that this "literary
fiction" of others described the reality of their relationship to
JHWH. "He does not need the covenant, but we need it. He
does not need our display of affection, but we need to display
it. He does not need our gifts, but we need to bring them. By
our dealings with our fellow vassals, we can fulfill our need and
thus manage a semblance of giving to him who needs nothing."
That line of reasoning may be a partial explanation for the development of the *decalogue*, the ten commandments, a distillation of the obligations incumbent on the people of Israel by
reason of their special relationship to JHWH.

The intimate relationship between liturgy, "dogma," and
ethics was much clearer to the people of the Old Testament
than it is to us. The liturgy re-enacts the great saving events of
the past when Jahweh met Israel in history. In those meetings
he revealed things about himself. And the nature of his revelation demanded a responding behavior. The Old Testament
goes further: The Divinity becomes angry when the proper response is not made.

A Jealous God

One of the notions that we find most difficult in the Old Testament flows from the notion of the jealous God. Exodus
quotes Jahweh as saying:

I the Lord am a wrathful God, visiting the iniquity of fathers on their children to the third and fourth generation

and showing mercy to the thousandth generation of them that love me (*Ex.* 20:5-6).

As a beginning, we might note that even by this harsh declaration, JHWH's mercy is about three hundred times as strong as his wrath (to the third generation . . . to the thousandth).

To some persons, this is not a satisfying answer.

They are more than ordinarily distressed by the jealous god (*el qn'*) of this passage and by the attribution of anger or wrath anywhere to God in the Old Testament. Is the idea of wrath in a god such a bad thing? To the metaphysical mind, the angry god presents problems. Anger represents a change or movement in emotions from one state to another. This distresses the student of metaphysics, since change is incompatible with perfection, and the student would see god as perfect.

Still, if the expression is at least partially mythic the expression of anger could still be an ethical consequent. The Old Testament presents its God as a person. What would our notion be of a person who impassively sees orphans defrauded, widows deprived, unjust wars won and innocent persons calumniated while the guilty are honored? Would not a real person grow angry at such sights? By using such language about JHWH the Old Testament only affirms its strong views about the divinity as a person.

Later in this book we shall talk about the role of the divine judge. (It is precisely as judge, though, that he becomes angry.) Here we prescind from the liturgical setting of his judgment, (in Psalm 82 he judges "in the assembly of the gods" [verse 1] and he judges on behalf of the poor and the fatherless [verses 3-4]. His wrath then is most easily stirred when the weak, the poor, the powerless are hurt. He becomes their mighty advocate and is angry with all who would harm them.) But his concern even here is not limited to the innocent. He is moved by the plight of those who are guilty. He is distressed by their guilt and would see them cleansed. This judgment flows from the Old Testament notion of morality as something that exists, not for the sake of JHWH, but for the sake of man. Immorality angers JHWH not because it deprives him of anything, but because it harms man, since it goes against the way in which man is constructed.

Their Sins to the Fourth Generation

No human being can commit a sin and prevent that sin from bringing harm to a later generation. This is terribly obvious in the world of the Old Testament. It is not so obvious to us. For this reason, we misunderstand the description of that god who will inflict punishment of sins on the third and the fourth generation after the sinner. We may ask: How is this possible? The Old Testament world would ask: Could it be otherwise? But is this idea really such a total puzzle to our age? Parents who engage in certain activities that seem objectively wrong (overindulgence in alcohol or other drugs) frequently find as the years go by that their children become a real burden to them. The children's lives are filled with emptiness; they suffer a special *angst* and finally they seek some release—through overindulgence in alcohol or other drugs.

All living Americans are descended from elders who lived in the pre-Civil War world (though many of us had elders who lived an ocean away from Fort Sumter). The adults of our great grand-parents' generation committed serious social sins. Who will deny that we are being punished today for sins that we did not commit and from which we have not really profited? It may be that some of us are being punished for sins that did not benefit our direct ancestors either. But it did profit some in their age. The sin of that profit—as sin so often is described in the Old Testament world—became a living thing, a living burden of guilt, a beast which lies in wait at the door (*Gen.* 4:7) and falls on the third and fourth generation.

This belief has been frequently understood and variously expressed throughout history. It is through the light of that experience that the church fathers—in a manner that puzzles or embarrasses us—saw "original sin" as something material that was passed on through the generative act, something which

made the sin universal (and the sex act vaguely shameful). The
Old Testament saw the same reality and phrased it differently.
Perhaps our own age has neither seen nor understood it. Nonetheless, *the human family is one.* For those who understand
this, there is really no such thing as personal, private sin.

Blessings That Extend to All

One of the sources of the "challenge and response" presentation of Old Testament theology is to be found in Exodus 20.
What we have here is a written version of an earlier liturgical
presentation. The presentation was simple but powerful. There
is a brief rehearsal of JHWH's benefits to the Hebrew people
with an appropriate pause for response. The response is trig-
gered by a repetition of the encapsulated sayings which, like
the decalogue, sum up the way in which Israel felt itself to be
called to respond to the Divinity. The text here (and in Deuteronomy 5) bears witness to a liturgy which at some point in
time followed a classic format which still lives (at least in the
West). There is a rehearsal of God's great deeds, and then the
question is asked (as in Ignatius' classic *The Spiritual Exer-
cises*) "What have I done for him? What am I doing for him?
What ought I do for him?" But the Old Testament liturgy had
its participants answer the question fairly simply by comparing
their private behavior with the community standard of the ten
commandments.

The decalogue is presented both in Exodus 20 and in Deuteronomy 5. Evidences of a liturgical dimension abound in
both texts, perhaps the outgrowth of something approximating
the introit psalm, as we mentioned in the preceding chapter. In
commenting on the decalogue, the viewpoint differs with each
commentator. So, realizing that our perspective is limited, we
may point out some few dimensions of this ethical distillation
that flows, perhaps, from centuries of earlier composition, and
which has affected all ethical thought in the West ever since.

We have already noted the intense *humanism* of the decalogue. It is concerned that man ought to act in a certain way, for

so he is made. This humanism asserts itself in a more striking fashion when the thunderclap of the Sabbath rest is commanded. It was an amazing breakthrough, that all men should have a day for leisure and for prayer. Both leisure and prayer have their proper place. (At least so the rabbis understood Exodus 20:8, and Deuteronomy 5:12—Remember the sabbath day *and* keep it holy.) But more astounding than the mere commandment of rest and prayer is that the Sabbath is commanded for all, "son, daughter, manservant, maidservant, ox, ass, cattle" (*Deut.* 5:14). The presumption is that the animals are to rest because they need supervision (or assistance) in order to work, and that will mean work for a man, ". . . and the stranger." The verse concludes with that last phrase. The Hebrew word used for "stranger" is *ger*. It is a poignant inclusion, because the *ger* is not a wealthy tourist. He is the poorest of all men in the ancient world. He is without any personal ownership of land and is without a nation. "You too were a slave in Egypt" (*Deut.* 5:15).

Perhaps no religious society can tolerate shabby treatment of the lowly, defenseless, and easily oppressed without discomfiture of conscience. (Although most societies, including religious ones, have frequently suppressed the stirrings of conscience.) But the Hebrew people would find it harder than others to mistreat the poor. Ever mindful of their own erstwhile *ger* status, they dealt with the poor with love and respect.

The poignancy of the helplessness felt by the *ger* (and a consequent appreciation of the mightiness in the Sinai revelation which liberated even him) is understood by modern travelers through Europe who have had some experience of the "guest-workers," as the euphemistic northern European expression has it. These are the landless. They flooded into Germany and Sweden in times of prosperity to work in factories. They have no passports, no citizenship in the country where they are working. They do not speak the language. They are alone. They work for lesser wages (though more than they could earn at home) until the advent of harder economic times. And then northern Europe tells them to return to Yugoslavia, to Turkey, to Greece, or to wherever they came from. And they pick up their few belongings and they go. They are *garim* (the plural of *ger*). It is easy to feel a sense of ethical superiority reading the above passage. America has no such phenomenon, we say. When hard times come, they come to all. But what of the American migrant workers? In any event, the message of Sinai extends to the lowest, the last and the least of all brethren. We too, the Hebrew people remind themselves, were *garim* in Egypt.

A Limited Monotheism

Elsewhere in this book we discuss Israel's progress toward monotheism, but one touching example of the time and effort which that progress demanded ought to be pointed out here. Consider the phrase: "No gods before my face" (*Deut.* 5:7). The Hebrew uses the phrase *'al panay*. Its precise meaning is not beyond dispute. But it can be claimed that this verse is not (as some have claimed) a later Hebrew preposition derived from a "broken-down" form of the expression "to my face." Rather, we have the archaic expression which means just that. Finally, since "before the face of" in Semitic language means "during his liturgy," this expression taken in itself means the following: "When the liturgy of JHWH is being celebrated, please do not bring images of other gods into the temple"!

Is it so shocking that the commandment asks only that other gods not be worshipped during Jahweh's liturgy? It shouldn't be. Israel was not always a mature adult. Hosea recalls the days "when Israel was a child . . ." (*Hos.* 11:1). One fascination for adults who work with children derives from the flashes of mature actions and thought which can be found in even the very young, admixed with childish behavior. If the decalogue as we have it is at all of one piece, the juxtaposition of a defense for the defenseless, a concern for landless *garim*, with this rather halting effort in the direction of monotheism is sheer delight. Geniuses are not brilliant all the time in everything. The Hebrews were religious geniuses. But on a given day, they thought that enough was being done if images of other gods should not be brought before JHWH while worship was going on. And from that unpromising beginning did the accomplishment of monotheism grow.

Do Not Kill—Except Sometimes

The decalogue does not forbid killing. It says, "You shall not commit *resah*" (*Deut.* 5:13 and *Ex.* 20:17), which forbids *murder* and *manslaughter.* In the Hebrew world, as in many worlds that have grown more ethically sensitive since, the elimination of human killing seemed not possible. War and violent death were concomitants of Hebrew life. Death as the ultimate punishment was accepted by the Hebrews as by their contemporaries. But *resah* was wrong. In other words, there was a limit to the kinds of justifiable killing.

Given this understanding, the commandment forbidding murder represented only small progress over the morality of the time. But the moral legislator—as the teacher—must begin where the student is. This law imposed restrictions to the kinds of justifiable killing. Unfortunately, the restrictions were not large in number, and in most societies they have increased only slightly since Sinai.

Some of the commandments in the decalogue are clear enough to the modern reader. There is no need to comment on them. But there are others which, although they were given valid interpretations by later religious communities, have lost some of their original sense. We shall look at two more of these.

"Do not take the name of the Lord . . ." (*Ex.* 20:7, *Deut.* 5:11). We spoke earlier about the Semitic belief in the power held by one who knows the name of another, and we pointed out that there is a parallel for it in our society. This commandment deals with the use of the name that is known. The Hebrew people knew the name JHWH, a name which other men did not know. The pastoral orator was concerned that this knowledge might be used improperly. He feared that the believing Hebrew might assume he has some power to control JHWH—which of course he does not—and may make a vain attempt to use that power, to invoke JHWH's strength against a personal enemy in improper fashion. Consequently, we have this commandment which might be translated, "Do not use the name of the Lord magically (*lashav*)."

"Do not covet" (*Ex.* 20:17, *Deut.* 5:21). "Covet" is the standard translation of the expression *hmd*. It is not totally clear that the Hebrew expression bears that freight easily. Perhaps the original expression, more than the English "covet," implied something more than mere desire for another's house or wife or whatever. So it should be honestly admitted that the meaning —whether simple longing or longing followed by action—is not clear. Christian readers will recall the commentary of the Matthaean church on this passage, "You have heard it said: do not commit adultery. I tell you that a man who looks lustfully at a woman has already committed adultery in his own heart" (*Mt.* 5:28). Did this early church remember Jesus calling his followers to a perfection more lofty than the Hebrew teaching, or did it remember him here, as so often, recalling his hearers to a perfection the Hebrew scriptures had long since proclaimed?

Scholars who study the decalogue in its present Old Testament setting differ on two serious points. Was the decalogue created in another foreign context and only later inserted into a kind of recital liturgy, or did the decalogue derive directly from a special kind of liturgy? We have discussed this earlier and will discuss it further in the last chapter of this book. Here, though, we can make one point of illustration from the New Testament memory. The gospel of Luke describes how Jesus was approached with a request: "Judge between me and my brother!" (*Lk.* 12:14). This Jesus refuses to do. The positing of the question, however, indicates a long tradition which accepts the religious leader as a judge with the wisdom to discern between X and Y and the authority somehow to enforce the results of his discernment. The specifics of this ancient tradition are not clearly known to us. Did the decalogue originate as the *Grágás* laws in Iceland, which flowed from a variety of individual decisions? Did the Old Testament priest, from his long experience of judging between man and man derive the courage to judge between man and God? Did the *rîb* pattern (the law-court model of dispute) so common in the prophets flow from this primitive judging activity? We do not know. I believe that the decalogue derived from an earlier liturgy. Scandinavian scholars had a valid insight when they projected the wandering judges of Iceland as useful comparisons with the creators of Israel's earliest legal tradition. Later Hebrew writers wrote up the conflict between God and man as though it were a dispute in a law court. We shall return to these ideas in the last chapter of this book. Here let us simply underline the long Hebrew tradition which sees the decalogue not as a burden, but as a gift from God. The faithful observance of the decalogue represents man's feeble efforts somehow to return the gift. People can exaggerate, however, the value of those feeble efforts. To counteract our tendency toward exaggeration, there was written the charming little story which occasioned the title of this chapter.

Jonah

To start with, let us explain the chapter title. The church of St. Luke urged its members to be faithful to all commandments, but cautioned, "When you have observed all that is commanded, still you must tell yourselves: we are idle servants and worthless; we did but our duty" (*Lk.* 17:10). Perhaps nowhere in the Old Testament is that message more powerfully and attractively preached than in the book of Jonah.

The book bears studying on several other grounds of course. It is ironic that this charming work has been the battleground of bitter conflicts between biblical scholars. It is a commonplace to observe that extremists lack a sense of humor. Some writing about Jonah lends unfortunate proof for that judgment.

Does It Matter If Jonah Is Historical?

The heart of the matter is really the above question. The first of the commentators to detect that Jonah was *didactic fic-*

tion should have been better pedagogues themselves. They might have begun their writing with solemn declarations that God indeed could have created a fish commodious enough to provide comfort for the traveling Jonah. Then they could have gone on to indicate their suspicions that he did not, that the work was one of charming entertainment, and that it taught through fiction (as the parables teach through fiction) a profound theological lesson. Inconveniently, the book of Jonah lacks a comforting tag-line which declares: "This is a parable; it is fictitious!" We have to figure it out for ourselves.

The reader might well pause here and read the few pages that make up the book of Jonah. Briefly summarized: A reluctant prophet is called by JHWH to preach repentance to the city of Nineveh. He attempts to flee his responsibilities through a sea voyage. God's wrath stirs up a mighty storm and non-Hebrew sailors, with some ethical reservations, finally cast Jonah overboard in an effort to appease his angry god. JHWH is appeased and sends a large fish who swallows Jonah comfortably alive. Jonah lives in the fish for three days and is vomited onto the shore of the land which needs his preaching. He preaches. They repent. Jonah is not happy about this, as he had looked forward to a violent destruction of the city. He sulks and grows quite angry with JHWH. He wanders into a desert area and would be destroyed by the sun, but is saved by the shade of a shrub which grows quickly enough to shelter him. And then the shrub begins to wither (attacked by a worm) and dies. Jonah makes intercessory prayer for the shrub, and God then chides him, pointing out that the affection which Jonah felt for a shrub, God felt for a city.

This cursory summary can make the book look childish and naive. Not so. It is delicately written in that layered construction with which our readers are now familiar. Hints are dropped on the delicate and fictitious nature of the work. Jonah in Hebrew means "dove" and is a frequent symbol for Israel. The word Nineveh, the city to which Jonah is sent, is written in Akkadian, the common language of Babylonia-Assyria, with pictographic signs that combine dwelling + fish. It does not take a cryptographic genius to see here allusion to the dove (Israel) dwelling in the house-of-fish or a reference to the Babylonian captivity. This clue, along with the argument from "Aramaisms" in the Hebrew text, leads scholars to date the book in post-exilic times when Old Testament writings began to be concerned with Israel's relationship to powerful gentile nations.

There is a two-edged reference to the myth of Chaos, the powers of darkness that live in general subservience to the Divinity. One flash from Chaos, the storm at sea, almost kills Jonah. Another, the great fish, at least an echo of the Leviathan myth, comes then to save him. (Leviathan, too, retains his powers, but he must generally obey the Divinity.) The great sea-monster serves the work of God just as the tiny shrub-destroying worm does. These poetic layers live just below the surface of the story about a silly and childish prophet.

God Loves All

The Old Testament religion has as much trouble in converting its adherents to a belief in universal salvation or God's universal love for all mankind as do most religions. Any religion must constantly war against the human question: What is in it for me? Most religious adherents answer this question by assuring themselves that their meritorious actions assure them of God's special love, while non-adherents remain "outsiders." The book of Jonah comes to terms with this very human and understandable bit of bad theology. All of the non-Hebrews in this work look pretty virtuous in comparison with Jonah. After all, he flees rather than obey a direct command of God. When a violent storm comes up at sea, he manages to fall asleep. The non-Hebrew sailors have some scruples about the direct taking of human life, while Jonah has none. The people of Nineveh do indeed repent when the word is preached to them and show this repentance in dramatic fashion with fast and sackcloth. In a remarkable failure for a prophet, Jonah becomes very disappointed at missing out on the sight of fire and brimstone and delivers himself of a line that may easily be paraphrased: "I knew it! I knew that it was going to turn out this way, and that is why I did not want to come here. Basically, you are a gracious god, slow to anger and quick to mercy. There is not much point in being a wrathful prophet who works for a god like you!"

If Jonah looks foolish in the work, it is for two reasons. The first we have often discussed: Much of scripture is composed with at least one eye on entertainment, and this humorous presentation is entertaining. Secondly, the authors of Jonah, through exaggeration, are reminding their readers or listeners, that much religious behavior can be silly and childish. We are called to keep the law. When we have done all that we ought, then we should remind ourselves that we still remain unprofitable servants. If we do not so remind ourselves, we may end up looking as foolish in the eyes of God as did the poor Jonah.

Later Jewish Thought

The world of the Old Testament was not always successful in grasping the lesson of Jonah. Later Jewish writing returned to this theme again and again, and in so returning frequently rewrote, edited, or commented on earlier Old Testament accounts. In a Broadway play of a few years back, *Hogan's Goat*, William Alfred rehearsed for a modern American audience a Christian-era Jewish legend which re-wrote the mighty victory of the Divine Warrior at the Reed Sea. "Horse and Chariot are thrown into the sea" (*Ex.* 15:1ff.). The noise and excitement bring the angels out from the inner chambers of heaven, and they lean precariously over the parapets, setting up a lusty cheer when now one horse, now one rider is covered by the foaming waves. Their cheering brings JHWH out of his study. He takes in the situation quickly and then rebukes them for their cheering at the sad disaster of the Egyptians, "Do you not know that the Egyptians are my children too?" he scolds sharply. And the shame-faced angels return to their heavenly chores inside the house.

The lesson is not easily learned. Once learned, it is very easily lost. The child is frightened by the notion that his parents also love his siblings. The religious adherent entertains an analogous fear. No matter how sternly his prophets may teach otherwise, he continues to hope that he *can* buy the God who cannot be bought through fidelity to the decalogue and later law. Perhaps in no Old Testament book (and in few books that come after the Old Testament) is the meritorious effect of the decalogue put into better focus than in the book of Jonah. It is a book written to scold not the sinner but the saint. He is reminded that "holiness" is a gift of God. If he looks to his fidelity to the decalogue as a proof of his virtue, he may ask himself the question, "Why do I obey? What are my inner motives?" A truthful answer to those questions may give him a feeling of greater kinship with the "sinner," the "outsider" or, if the questioner is a pious Hebrew, with the gentile.

The New Testament, in the gospel of Luke, reminds people of this lesson in the parable of the elder brother (*Lk.* 15:25-32). This is the second half of the parable of the so-called prodigal son. The elder brother of the prodigal grieves that the lost have been found and that the dead have come to life. The weakness of the elder brother, the saved, the saint, is always with us. Perhaps for that reason, the book of Jonah—for all its brevity —soon found a place in the lectionary of the early church.

8
On Death
and Theologizing

Bang the Drum Slowly, a novel of the fifties, came to life on the screen in the seventies. It skirted, generally successfully, the maudlin, while giving an account of a journeyman major-league baseball player who finds himself dying at the beginning of a baseball season. There is strong contrast in the story. The usually rugged good health of professional athletes, and the birth of a child to one of them, are pictured against the overriding presence of the dying man. The narrator of the tale accounts for what goodness he finds among men in this fashion: Everybody knows that everybody else is dying too. That's why they sometimes try to be nice.

The world of the Old Testament was a world where—unlike our own—death was ever present to the living. The brevity of life-span and the possibility of early death even by natural causes were accepted facts. Moreover the high likelihood of death by violence, in single combat or in war, was a part of everyday life in Old Testament times, just as traffic accidents and industrial pollution in the air belong to ours. But for the people of Israel there was an added dimension to the problem of death. And that was the problem they themselves caused, the deaths that they inflicted in hewing out a new nation. Remember, we have stressed up to now that the Old Testament represents a steadily growing ethical mentality. A simpler stratum of the Old Testament composition viewed the land of Israel as a "gift of God." As the message of Sinai and its implications grew clearer, the more sensitive among the Hebrews felt a growing need to cope with the ethical problems that the elimination of the "Jebusites, Hivites, Amorites, Girgashites, and Perizzites" presented to the conscience.

Some may object that merely to raise such ethical issues is an anachronism, that we are retrojecting a twentieth-century problem into the ancient world. Surely the American preoccupation with the ethical problems of dislocating Indians did not seem much to slow down "manifest destiny." There may be some validity to such objections. On the other hand, the legislation which flowed from Sinai, purporting to point out in ever greater detail the finer points of the divine will, shows us that the Hebrew people were preoccupied with religious (and consequently moral) questions to a degree that has not been characteristic of the American people in any century. (In fact, there is evidence that throughout the history of the white man in North America there were many who scrupled over the problems of the Indian. Lewis Hanke, in *The Spanish Struggle for Justice in the Conquest of America* [Little, Brown, 1965], makes a case for those Spanish theologians who were concerned to follow the conquest with "Christian and just principles." Rev. F. P. Prucha, in his *Documents of United States Indian Policy* [University of Nebraska Press, 1975], cites considerable evidence for such ethical concern on the part of later Americans. He quotes Henry Knox, our first secretary of war, who wrote in 1789, "The Indians being the prior occupants possess the right of the soil." And Senator Frelinghuysen, who spoke in the Senate to oppose a bill which would remove Indians from certain territories: "Where is the decree or ordinance that has stripped these early and first lords of the soil?")

Is there any evidence that some of the pious Hebrews, like so many brave men who have followed them, did not really fear death but feared being murderers? Did they have to come to terms with this? The impression is that they did and that their scruples were of a nature that is fairly universal with societies that have developed any conscience at all.

Such problems belong not simply to the professional soldier. Robert Viscott in *The Making of a Psychiatrist* apologizes for his sense of humor which borders, he admits, on that of the smart aleck. He found early in his medical career, he says, that he simply could not handle the emotional implications of being involved in the death and dying process, adding perhaps to patients' pain in his efforts to help, and so he turned quickly to gallows-humor as a kind of release.

If the physician or politician in our society feels such distress and the need of coping with it, is it unreasonable to find an entire nation enwrapped in schizophrenia while dealing with the problems of war? It was as a result of the pain in that schizophrenia that the Hebrew people developed what might be called a "theology of conquest."

Some of the themes involved in this theology appear elsewhere in our book. Here we would stress that the motif of the Divine Warrior plays a dominant role in this thinking because the people of Israel need a way of coming to emotional grips with the problems of being killers. The Divine Warrior, remember, is the powerful ancient god who battles mightily for his people. In the famous passage in the book of Numbers 10:34-36, we find a layer which treats the warrior in very simple fashion. He lives in a box which is brought to the site of battle. When the battle commences, he is told simply, "Rise!" and he does that. When he has won the battle, he is told, "return, relax." And he does. The Divine Warrior is personally involved in the battle because *these are his enemies*. The last line of Psalm 137 which horrifies us, "Blest be he who takes your infants and dashes them against rocks," becomes almost tolerable in the theology of conquest. The god's enemies deserve to die and to leave no posterity.

Anything "primitive" about the god-that-lives-in-a-box was tolerated by a later age, precisely because of its steadily growing need for a cohesive theology of conquest. The Divine Warrior is accepted, not simply by reason of the mythic values we described elsewhere, but also because he plays a vital role in legitimizing the deaths required by conquest. Perhaps an earlier age found no ethical problems in it; a later age found considerable problems and so continued to mythologize the gruesome activity.

Let us make clear what we are about here. We are engaged in no defense of the brutality that lies strewn throughout much of the Old Testament. There is a fundamental inconsistency between the loftiest teachings of the Sinai message and the way that the Hebrews lived for much of the biblical period. And they saw that more clearly than do we. Moreover, they had to live with it, to reach some kind of separate peace with their consciences on the issue of killing. The Divine Warrior theology was an effort to make that separate peace possible. A life of pacifism was simply not open to them. Even the brutality of cheering on infant slaughter (as in Psalm 137) had an awful logic to it. Potential enemy soldiers are more easily attacked in the cradle than anywhere else. The problems of the theology of conquest sharply reveal the distinction between exegesis (the study of the meaning of the text for original audiences) and hermeneutics (the meaning of the text for us who read today). In this chapter, we are reading only as exegetes.

The Ban and the Dwelling of the God

The expression *ḥrm* with the meaning of "the ban" occurs (in variant forms) about forty times in the prose of the Old Testament. The history of the word is itself interesting. Its basic meaning seems to be "to set apart, to consecrate." In fact, it rapidly comes to mean to destroy utterly. To put something or someone "under the ban" means to mark it or him for destruction. The manner in which the ban is exercised leaves the modern reader somewhat puzzled. In 1 Samuel 15, for example, we read that Saul and his people did indeed wipe out an enemy on one occasion. They spared the King (Agag), for reasons that are not clear, and the best of his livestock. Saul alleges in his defense that the beasts were being saved for special sacrifice to the Lord. With the approval of the narrating voice of 1 Samuel, the prophet tells Saul that he has lost favor with the Lord (verse 22ff.). And Saul does not regain it, though he cheerfully summons Agag and slaughters him "before the Lord in Gilgal"—an expression which leaves the suspicion that some type of liturgical human sacrifice was not unknown among the Hebrews.

Ḥrm then came to mean at least two things. "Set apart" and "destroyed"; this last meaning was at least occasionally envisioned as the means by which the thing destroyed is thus "set apart" for the Lord. In the theology of conquest, it becomes enough finally that the thing or person simply be destroyed and the *ḥrm* is fulfilled.

It is interesting to note that Mount Hermon, from the same root (*ḥrm*) in Semitic, is the "dwelling of the god" in some texts which pre-date the Hebrew Bible. Hermon in the Old Testament too is the sacred mountain and dwelling of the gods. It may be, of course, that there is no more connection between these words *ḥrm* and *hermon* than that both are somehow "set apart." One can at least wonder out loud at the possibility that *ḥrm* type destruction is special to worshippers of the god who dwells on *hermon*.

Theologizing in the Old Testament

The Old Testament itself does not give us a clear idea of which authors articulated notions like these. It does not tell us much about early Hebrew "theologians." Yet, in the presumption that at least some of the theologians came from cultic religious personnel, there are clues offered by literature outside the Old Testament. We speak elsewhere in this book of the sacredness of the "act of entering" which became historicised by the entry into the promised land. Other echoes can be found in the sacred role of the high priest who enters the sanctuary and, in the New Testament, in praise of Christ the Eternal High Priest precisely because he performs the "act of entering" once and for all. As so frequently, the world of cult imitates the divine world. As the priest enters the sanctuary, as the liturgical procession (so described) of the holy people enters the land, so the divine son enters "heaven." Since all this is clearly known, it is more than interesting that one of the Ugaritic texts describes cultic personnel as *'rbm*, the "enterers."

We alluded earlier in the book to the city of Ugarit, and we shall do so again. The importance of Ugarit for Old Testament studies is difficult to exaggerate. It is, as we said, a vital witness to the kind of language used by the Hebrews in the thirteenth century B.C. It is the only significant witness to the kind of theologizing being done in that part of the world occupied by the earliest Hebrews. Moreover, it is an excellent witness to the kind of theologians encountered by Israel when it conquered the city of Jerusalem. Those theologians eventually helped them to formulate their theology of conquest.

Commonalities between Hebrew and non-Hebrew theologians are easy to enumerate. We previously cited the non-Hebrew (Ugaritic) belief that the sanctuary somehow "equalled" heaven. The Hebrew (in *Ps.* 11:4) says bluntly:

> JHWH sits in his Holy Temple,
> JHWH's throne is in heaven.

So in a certain sense, to be in the sanctuary is to be in heaven. How successful were the Hebrews in articulating the nature of that certain sense? Not much more successful than we twentieth century theologians. Perhaps, though, the Hebrews were somewhat advantaged over later and more reflective societies. Because they were not compelled to articulate the metaphysical compatibility between presence in the temple and presence in the divine realm, they could use lines like the above without restraint. Similarly, it was easier for such people to see a Divine Warrior defeating both chaos and the Hivites.

The chronological sequence of myth and reality is not spelled out in the Old Testament. The general pattern seemed to be as follows: A real event occurred. Decades (or even centuries) later, the Hebrew people, while reflecting on that event and seeking a way to transmit its significance to their children, saw a relationship between the event and the hoary myths that antedated the event. In regard to the theology of conquest, the Hebrew people had absorbed a certain mythology from their priests who were descendants of the pre-Canaanite priesthood. So the Hebrews used a pre-Hebrew myth to explain what happened in the conquest.

Those who participated in the conquest, those who were on

the scene, had no need of ethical justification and hence of mythologizing. Pacifism was never a real option to them; their options were to inflict destruction or to endure it. A later age, bathed in the ethical glow of Sinai's lightning, began to question. For them, the process of mythologizing began again, as in so many other Old Testament themes. The Divine Warrior of Canaanite legend was reexamined; the Hebrew battles for conquest and new land were retold; activities of heaven and earth were reintegrated. And a viable theology of conquest was born.

Ironically, much background required for the formulation of that conquest-theology was taken from the conquered people. The monumental three-volume work of Mitchell Dahood, S.J., on the psalms left much controversy, stemming from the relationship he saw between the Hebrew language and the earlier Ugaritic. Certainly, Dahood made one thing clear: The Ugaritic material is extremely useful for *elucidation* of older Hebrew. This term "elucidation" sidesteps the question of how closely allied the Ugaritic material and the older Hebrew is. Interpreted in light of the Ugaritic, the older Hebrew frequently makes sense where, without such interpretation, it sometimes does not make sense. On grounds of sheer pragmatism, then, this procedure seems to have something in its favor.

No one has accused Dahood of not going far enough in his imaginative intuitions about the *grammatical* relationships he finds between the Ugaritic and Hebrew materials. Occasionally, though, he stops short of pointing out the *theological* inheritance which Israel had from the world of Ugarit. For example, he correctly translates a difficult Hebrew phrase in Psalms 48:3 as "the heart of *Zpn*" and notes that Mount Zion is so described. The word *Zpn*, as we already noted, has come generally to mean "north" in Hebrew. But its older meaning, "the sacred mountain," "the dwelling of the god," is sometimes preserved. What Dahood does not note here is the possibility that Zion is described as the "heart of Zpn" so that the pious Hebrew will not be offended by reference to *Zpn*—a pagan shrine of Ugarit. This is a reminder that so much of the Psalmic theology is derived from Canaanite (echoed in the Ugaritic) sources. A later editor tells his hearers that Zion is the heart of *Zpn*. That whatever is the best of *Zpn* is now represented in Mount Zion where the God of Israel dwells alone.

One last example of Ugaritic form and Hebrew spirit may suffice as a connection to the last part of this chapter—a brief discussion of the complexities involved with the history of the Hebrew priesthood. This discussion should be profitable because it will tell us something about the "theologians" who developed the theology of conquest. Secondly, the action of the priesthood in "punishing bad Hebrews" is intimately related to the defence of violence offered by the theology of conquest.

The "Good News" in Ugarit

The Old Testament in Hebrew frequently (but not always) used the intensive root of *bsr* to mean "proclaiming good news." For example, the beautiful feet of the messenger in Isaiah 52:7 belong to him who *bsr* good news and "causes people to hear" about peace. It is of more than casual interest that later Arabic, with all the conservatism which we have mentioned as belonging to Arabic, uses a root from *bsr* to translate the *euangelion*, the gospel, or "good news" of the Greek language. Ugaritic text 76 uses the term *bsr* when proclaiming the good news that "a wild ox is born, yes a buffalo to him that rides on the clouds." The Ugaritic text 77 speaks of "a virgin that will conceive." Prescinding for the moment from the meaning of that text for the people of Ugarit, once that meaning is known, we shall be in a better position to discuss the meaning of the text in Isaiah 7:14 that speaks also of a virgin that will become pregnant. While these few lines have been singled out, the Ugaritic material is replete with the literary structures which were to win immortality through the Hebrew texts of the Old Testament and the subsequent Greek texts of the New Testament. This much is clear: The modes of much Old Testament theological speech are directly derived from styles used by the theological composers of Ugarit. From our knowledge of the customs in the ancient Near East, we know that cultic figures had much to do with the origins of this sort of material. It is difficult not to conclude that some cultic leaders came directly into Hebrew religious worship and brought some of their literary and stylistic forms with them to use in the employ of their newly accepted God—the God of the Hebrews.

There is no question that the origins of Hebrew priesthood are murky and complex. Part of the confusion and contradiction that the Old Testament brings to its descriptions of the origins may be due to simple ignorance. A given writer just did not know how the priesthood developed. Part of it, surely, may belong to the *pietas* dynamic—the writer did know, but he is embarrassed by his knowledge. His simple fathers came in from the desert and were much impressed by the cultivated priests of the city and so they hired them away from other gods. The great grandson wishes that it had been otherwise, and that a "theology of conquest" had been developed without any "foreign" help.

Priests, Levites, and a Rewriting of History

At least part of the reason for the confusion which the Old Testament affords on the origins of its priesthood is to be found in that explanation. Later generations were aware of how much theology a "modern, foreign priesthood" brought into Israelite worship with them, and the later age was embarrassed by this notion, so they obscured it. Part of the confusion is due to the normal amount of historical confusion. The age to which the origins of priesthood were clear did not bother to keep terribly straight accounts. It was no problem for them. By the time that it became a problem, historical memory was shaky.

The relationship between the terms "priest" and "levite" is not clear. In light of all that we have seen about tradition criticism, this is hardly surprising. The subject of priests is treated by the D source, by the book of Ezekiel, by the P source, and by the chronicler (the presiding "editor" of Chronicles, Ezra, and Nehemiah). Each of these works had a different perspective.

Perhaps most surprising of all, is that the term *ger* is so often associated with the levite (Cf., e.g., *Deut.* 16:14). With all that we have said before about the role of the *ger,* it is puzzling to see the levite in this role. He is associated with the landless (*Deut.* 10:9). While it is a consolation, that the "Lord himself is his inheritance," in fact, this is a polite way of describing the levite as landless. And this in a society where ownership of land was the only real indication of any wealth at all. But in some periods, apparently, the levite had something more than wealth going for him. The "wandering cleric" of Judges 17 finds employment fairly easily. The owner of the house is delighted that his private shrine will be manned by an authentic levite. So there was something unique about the priestliness of the levite in this memory. His poverty and landlessness, his general *ger* status did not prevent his coming with dignity onto a new scene.

There is a further allusion to the connection between priesthood and a theology of conquest. Genesis 49 presents in the blessing of Jacob an ancient memory which chastises Simeon and Levi (verse 5) as "instruments of cruelty to their brethren." This is a vague allusion to an ancient test in which Levi and Simeon stood at the side of the embattled god and slew the brethren who had somehow violated his good pleasure. And yet another ancient song views this same memory differently. Deuteronomy 33 praises Levi, and awards the Thummim and Urim to him (the priestly instruments of oracular power) because he was tested at Massah and at Meribah (verse 8) and showed no mercy to his own brethren nor to his children. He said of them, "I do not know them" (verse 9). And so did he observe the word of the Lord and keep his covenant. The last chapter in our book discusses this memory from another viewpoint. Here let us note that there was a conflict in darkly ancient times. There was a good side and a bad side in this conflict. Some memory places the levites on the right side of the conflict. (Perhaps even the memory of Genesis 49 does not place them on the wrong side, but remembers with sadness their role in the chastisement inflicted on the brethren.) The rewriting of these episodes by Hebrew editors is analogous to their "theology of conquest." Sadness over necessary violence in the past permeates both.

Some Old Testament writing on the subject of priests and levites is simply an effort to find a "parentage" for the priesthood of a later day. (There may be an analogy in modern politics. A contemporary Democrat or Republican—despite the complexity of modern issues—attempts honestly to find in Jefferson or in Lincoln a political "ancestor.") When we come to discuss the "judgment cult" in the last chapter, our current suggestion may make a bit more sense. But if the last redactor of, let us say, Deuteronomy 33, knew of a contemporary role for the levite as "judge," he would find it easy to associate him with an ancient theological memory of the stern warriors who separated the good from the bad at the waters of Meribah.

For the book of Deuteronomy, priests and Levites are the same. Generally, the book of Ezekiel, the *P* source, and the chronicler distinguish between them. Moreover, the theologies of these sources differ. For example, *P* deals with a god who makes possible a "theology of appearance." The theophany is direct and real. God is seen. The *D* source is more restrained. It deals with a theology of the name. God's "name" is present, not precisely his reality. So the *D* source represents a more reflective type of theology than the *P*. Could we argue then that the relationship between priest and levite which *D* offers is also more reflective?

Some have suggested that the confusion in the accounts of priests and levites arises in part from two later reforms: that of Hezekiah (715-) and Josiah (640-). (The period between them is almost insignificant; the reform became the work of the ongoing bureaucracy which administered governments as kings came and went.) One of the major problems of such reforms was the conflict between the city priesthood (at Jerusalem and largely derived from non-Hebrew origins) and the "country priesthood." The latter originated when Israel was a loose confederation. Its historical roots go back to an earlier time, when the emerging nation revolved around a central shrine—other than Jerusalem. Moreover, with the passage of time and with the amalgamation of new tribes, the number of shrines multiplied. A united nation demanded a single shrine —that of Jerusalem. However the livelihood of the country priests demanded continuation of local worship. The reforms of which we are speaking brought the country priests to the city, gave them a role—albeit a lesser one—in temple worship, and guaranteed them an income.

The reform was not an easy one for Hezekiah and Josiah—if reform is ever easy. Nostalgia and conservatism were against them. Although generations had passed since the integration of the central shrine priesthood, it was not complete. The levites represented the ancient traditions; they were the "natives." The non-levites were the usurpers, innovators, and foreigners. Still, Josiah was not deterred. 2 Kings 23 tells how the local shrines were amalgamated; the local priests were given a share in stipends and thus their living was assured.

The mysteries of the relationship between priest and levite remain largely unsolved. For Deuteronomy, the priests and the levites have virtually the same function; it is to carry the ark. But there are some intriguing possibilities that leave room for speculation. Deuteronomy 33:10 gives pride of place to the levitical role of *judging* and *teaching* (the two "liturgies" which are discussed in our last chapter) and only after that, the burning of incense and the offering of sacrifice. The book of Micah upbraids some kind of priesthood precisely for its preoccupation with *money* gotten for teaching. Of the three groups singled out for blame, the "heads" are scolded for taking money for *judging*, the "prophets" for divination, and the priests for "teaching." At least one possible interpretation of this verse is that there was one priesthood which existed primarily for *teaching* and not sacrifice. One last complexity of the relationship is pointed up by the line in Ezekiel referring to "the sons of Zadok who alone among the sons of Levi. . . ." A good case can be made for identifying Zadok as the non-Hebrew priest par excellence. This line in Ezekiel then would be one further effort to accommodate the relationship between these two priesthoods.

The references, though, to teaching and to sacrifice as disparate priestly acts are intriguing since they make fairly easy a reference to disparate priesthoods. Is the teaching role really such an ancient priestly one? (A good argument in favor of that is precisely that the references we find are "throw-away lines" when the author is talking apparently about something else.) Or is the development of the role of priestly-teacher something late? Perhaps it was a role which the country priests took to themselves when compelled to come to the temple by various reforms, when they were given a salary, some leisure, but no real function that compared in dignity to the one which they left at the small shrines back home? Is the work of Deuteronomy, as we have it, really derived from such a teaching priesthood? Was the development of a theology of conquest from primitive memories the work of such a priesthood? Could any priesthood have developed the theology of conquest as we have it without using mythic teaching inherited from an earlier conquered priesthood?

On Facing the Truth

In fact, of course, we do not know the answer to many of the above questions. It is for this reason that we dare to have recourse to analogies from a universal human dynamic. The Hebrew people in the age of Hezekiah and Josiah were given some periods of leisure and respite from the struggle to build the nation. While forces continued to threaten them from outside, they were just that—external enemies. The inner enemy was no more. Israel was a united nation. Jebusites, Hivites, and other analogous people would no longer survive, except as they were blended into the Hebrew nation. It was only in such times and under such circumstances that a nation could afford the leisure of reflecting on how all this had come to pass. As a gift of such time and leisure (for any reflective thought requires much of both) was born the final redaction that described the theology of conquest.

9
Jerusalem—
The One of Gold

Both Jew and Arab—to the anxiety of the entire world—grow somewhat frantic about the beauties of Jerusalem. This puzzles many tourists. If one has grown up in the changing scenery of Massachusetts, viewed the rustic hills of North Wilbraham, and walked along the shore at Gloucester, Jerusalem's beauty seems much oversold. There is a sameness to it. Its climate is sometimes described by Israeli natives as "fantastic!" but that is only in comparison with the climate throughout the rest of Palestine.

The late great Rabbi Abraham Heschel wrote a short book on Jerusalem (*Israel: an Echo of Eternity*, 1967). With rich poetic language it described what walking through the city meant to Heschel who was even then an old man. With eloquence that cannot be described but only quoted, he kept saying things like: "We, a people of orphans, have entered the walls to greet the widow of Jerusalem and the widow is a bride again. She has taken hold of us, and we find ourselves at the feet of the prophets. We are the harp, and David is playing."

For someone who had lived more than two years in Jerusalem and who considers himself more an intellectual than a poet, such outbursts were hard sayings. It was with the reading of Fritz Stolz's *Strukturen und figuren im Kult von Jerusalem* (Berlin, 1970) that the intellectual basis of Heschel's poetry started to come together. And that basis lay very close to something which has been at the core of the present book: the conviction that most of the Old Testament grew from dialogue—between prophet and people, between king and scholar, or, in

99

Jerusalem, between Jebusite and Hebrew. Stolz feels, as we do, that God reveals mediately.

When we use that expression, we are not denying that God could speak to man face-to-face. We are not even saying that he has never done so. What we are rather stressing is that in the normal course of events he reveals through other modes. He uses the imagination, or he uses the touch of other men to teach us. Why is this so? We do not know of course. But perhaps by calling us to use our imagination, he reminds us no matter how closely he calls us to share his life, that we are indeed human, for only humans imagine. By teaching us through other men, especially men who are much separated from us in time and custom, he reminds us that all men are brothers.

There was a time-frame in Hebrew history when the nation had a variety of beautiful and powerful experiences—even though they didn't remember them perfectly: the Exodus event, the Sinai event, perhaps the announcing of stipulations. But it was only in Jerusalem that all this came together in a synthesis which holds—largely—to the present day. For this reason, pious Jews prayed the world over as they got ready to open the ark and to take out the Torah:

> Merciful Father:
> Deal kindly with Zion.
> Rebuild the walls of Jerusalem.

For it was in Jerusalem that the synthesis of historical memory was shaped and inserted into a religious tradition that already existed.

Is This Syncretism?

Much writing done in recent years has been intent on showing a kind of *syncretism* in the Old Testament, a blurring of religious lines, a mingling and confusion of thought. Because so many of the externals in what came to be mainstream Hebrew religion are found in the Canaanite world, some scholars have argued that demarcations which earlier scholars had found between the two worlds are false. Yet when this book speaks of *mediated revelation* it does not refer to syncretism.

If any proof is needed of the difference between *spirit* and *forms* of religious worship, one example may suffice. The Christian eucharist is derived from a Jewish meal. Its most intensely Christian point, the words of consecration, "This is my body," is derived from a Jewish exclamation, "This is the bread of affliction. . . ." What has happened here, as so often in religious history, is that old beauty has been given new meaning.

It is difficult to recall from religious history a more powerful example of that transformation than the religio-cultural experience which took place when Hebrews met Jerusalem. The relationship of Islam to Jerusalem, which will be discussed in this chapter, is easier to document, since historically it is much closer to our own day. For a variety of reasons, though, it is not easy to discuss. The compatibility between the intellect and religious feeling in Islam is uneasy. For this reason, the greatest of Western scholars in Islamics described (with an infelicitous phrase) the golden age of Arabic philosophy as "an excrescence upon the face of Islam." It was badly put. He did mean though that philosophical reflection did not fit with the rest of the whole. Nonetheless, we shall attempt some reasoned analysis of Islam and Jerusalem before we finish.

A pre-Hebrew text from the 1400's gives the name of Jerusalem as *uru-shulman*, which might be interpreted as "city or temple of *shulman.*" The intimacy with which the name of the divinity is bound up with the subsequent history of Israel is clear. The stern prophet, Nathan, who would have none of this "corrupting" that cultural contact with Jerusalem involved, called David's son "Jedidja," the "darling of Ja," but David— and history—have called him *Solomon.* (Cf. 2 *Sam.* 12:24.)

The name Solomon, of course, is fairly clearly derived from *Shulman.* But *Shulman* is not alone the god of Jerusalem. (For the non-Semitist, it should be emphasized here that the triliteral root of the two names *šlm* is the same. The *an* in *Shul-*

man is a noun-formation ending.) What we do not know very much about is the relationship among the various gods which Jerusalem worshipped. For example, the appearance of the names Adoni*zedek* and Melchi*zedek* as king-names for Jerusalem, coupled with the role of Zadok in the post-Jerusalem Hebrew religion, points to the high likelihood of a divinity *Zdk* in Jerusalem history. Zadok becomes most prominent after the accession of Solomon. Prior to that he had only shared the prominence of Abiathar, the royal high priest. Did the erstwhile Jedidja share a higher tolerance for the gods of Jerusalem than did his father? This could be at least partially an explanation of Zadok's rise to power.

The name *Zdk* presents some intriguing possibilities again of ideas that predated Hebrew Jerusalem and lived on through Muslim Jerusalem. We have mentioned elsewhere in the book the possibility of a "cult of judgment" that underlies much of the Old Testament, and we shall discuss it a bit further in the final chapter of this book. Here we would add the following. The Hebrew text carries references to *ain mišpat* (fountain of judgment) and *beer šeba'* (court of swearing), *massah* (testing), *meribah* (dispute) in its most ancient strata. For a variety of reasons, it can be suggested that these are references to an ancient cult by which decisions were rendered, that this cult became itself a model for the relationship between God and man, the so-called *rîb* pattern or dispute-model found in the prophets.

The "Uppsala school" of Old Testament scholarship would be comfortable with the movement from judgment cult to *rîb* pattern. It is one of the basics of this school that those actions which take place in the cult take place also in "Heaven."

To 'what happens' in the cultic drama corresponds what happens in heaven; he that sits enthroned in the Temple is the one who sits enthroned up there, and sends thunder and rain and 'renews the surface of the earth' and with awe, all kings and peoples ought to recognize that he is at the same time the god of Israel.

So writes Sigmund Mowinckel in *The Psalms in Israel's Worship* (I, p. 174). This is a common notion among scholars influenced by the Uppsala school.

This view is not without analogies in Jewish sources. Heschel cites (p. 147) Rabbi Yochanan of the third century who wrote, "The Holy One, Blessed Be He, said: 'I will not enter heavenly Jerusalem until I can enter earthly Jerusalem.' "

Zdk means "justice" or "righteousness." Stolz sees this function as a part of the cosmic realm; the God who is warrior and who defeats chaos is also the cosmic judge, bringing about "right order." This is certainly true, but it by no means eliminates a "cult of judgment." In fact, it almost calls for it, for what happens in the arena of cosmic conflict, where the gods live, should have a cultic echo here on earth. Whatever else the school of St. Matthew meant, the notion of binding and loosing taking place on earth and being felt in heaven derives from a long, long religious tradition (*Mt.* 18:18). The fact that this tradition is also associated with "judgment" is significant for our purposes, as is the fact that the major inscription over the Rock in Omar's mosque reads: "Pardon the sinner who comes here." The notion of the liturgy of judgment permeates the Old Testament and is prominent in the city of Jerusalem.

Arabic legends cited in Haldane's *Jerusalem* are interesting at this juncture. The "Mosque of the Chain" is built in the general area of the Temple site. The chain there honored is explained by a variety of tales. The chain was put there by David or ·by Solomon to assist in the making of proper judgments. It reached to Heaven and was attached to a bell. If the plaintiff deserved it, the bell would ring and his request would be granted. Or the chain was so fashioned that the man in the right, no matter how short, could reach it. The man in the wrong, no matter how tall, could not.

Because of this "confusion" between the dwelling of the god and the sanctuary of earth, Sura (chapter) 17 of the Koran proves the Muslim love for Jerusalem. The chapter describes Mohammed's miraculous flight to "the furthest mosque." Muslim theologians insist that this refers to Jerusalem. Non-

Muslim commentators suggest that the site was heaven. But once Jerusalem became a sanctuary, in one valid sense Jerusalem *was* heaven for the pious Mohammedan—as for the pious Jew.

The etymology of *uru-shulman* is not totally clear. The earlier translation, "temple of *shulman*" which we offered is tenable. It is derived, however, not precisely from *uru-shulman* but from a much longer version of the name which occurs in pre-Hebrew material. It has been suggested that *uru* is derived from the common Semitic root *yrh* with the meaning "oracle, decision, wisdom." (This brings an explanation for the oak of *Moreh* [derived from the same root] which occurs in Genesis 12:6, 35:4, 35:8, and Deuteronomy 11:30. It would be translated "the oak of decision." To this day, the picture of the Arab chieftain seated under a shade tree and settling disputes is a common one.) Also interesting is that one of the other major gods of Jerusalem, *El*, appears in the Hebrew bible in connection with the "well of swearing." In fact, a noted biblical scholar, W. Zimmerli, sees *el olam* as the major god connected with that site.

For Stolz, the god of Jerusalem is judge (with the differences we have noted); he is the battler against chaos and the warrior against one's enemies. These last two are not unrelated. The same god who defeated chaos, gives "the enemies of Abraham into his hand" (*Gen.* 14:20). So does the earlier stratum see the Divine Warrior. Chaos upsets right order, so the Divinity must subdue it. Our enemies upset the right order, so JHWH must subdue them. The fact, however, that the Divine Warrior motif continued to live and thrive long after this early period is due to its responding to a later deep need; hence our theology of conquest.

Jerusalem and Sacrifice

In the various traditions of Jerusalem geography, there are some discrepancies. Still, in one old tradition, Mount Moriah is the name for the temple site and the location of the Holy of Holies. Of this Heschel writes:

> Why was Mount Moriah chosen to be the site on which to build the Temple and the Holy of Holies rather than Mount Sinai on which the Ten Commandments were given? The answer offered is that Mount Moriah was the site where Abraham sacrificed his beloved son and the sanctity of sacrifice transcends the sanctity of the Commandments.

This is a remarkable statement for a rabbi, that sacrifice (even of Isaac) can be greater than the sanctity of the commandments. What is even more remarkable is that this attitude is somewhat shared by the traditions of Islam.

It is not totally clear why Jerusalem came to play such a great role in the religion of Islam. As we have noted, there is a certain uneasiness between Islam and intellectual inquiry (which does not make Islam unique among religions). One of the results of this has been a lack of scientific study of the Koran comparable to the study of the Old Testament.

Mohammed began with the notion that Jerusalem would be central for his religion. The *kibla*, the direction in which the pious were to turn while reciting their prayers, was originally toward Jerusalem. And in most Arab legends the popular explanation was that Jerusalem and Moriah were the site of Abraham's offer to sacrifice Isaac. Abraham has a most honored role in Islam. He is the *khalil allah*, the "friend of God." This praise is only slightly suspect. Islam has some of the same difficulties with Judaism that Christianity has with it. If Judaism is perfect, then what role is there for the later religion? Islam resolved this problem by concluding that the Hebrew religion had become "too exclusive," but was to be praised for the purity of its monotheism. That monotheism Islam would recover and would universalize.

Moreover, Islam understood Jerusalem as the place where it all came together for the Hebrews. If monotheism is what reli-

gion is all about (and to the Muslims it really was) then Jerusalem can only be *al quds*, "the holiness." Whatever the pre-
history of Jerusalem was—and surely the pious Muslim would
be shocked by much of what we have written here—it was in
Jerusalem that the Hebrews put the finishing touches to that
perfect monotheism which they then proceeded to mar by their
"exclusivity!" (For the Muslims, Christianity became universal but then corrupted monotheism.)

"Peaceful Conquest" of Jerusalem

We have mentioned the "peaceful taking" of Jerusalem by
David. It is at least interesting to compare this with the Arabic
description of the approach to Jerusalem by the Caliph Omar
(638 A.D.) who was resolved (the taking of the city being assured) that there be no bloodshed. Arab legend has em-
bellished this considerably. The man is described as "simple
and devout," wearing "ordinary raiment" and "redolent of
humility." Such a person approached the Patriarch Sophronius
and explained what the new order of things was to be, even as
David approached the Jebusite leadership of Jerusalem, (the
"priest-king" *Zadok*?) and won it over to his new order.

The Old Testament refers to a divine manifestation which
has become *mal'ak JHWH*, a messenger of the Lord, (and in
fact an angel of punishment if not judgment) in our "expurgat-
ed version" of the story (2 *Sam.* 24:16). It is by reason of this
manifestation that David purchased "the threshing floor of
Araunah the Jebusite." There is no need to rehearse the arguments here for a threshing floor as cultic center. Here we
would point out that Araunah is a faintly disguised version of
Uranos, the Indo-European form of the god's name. This fur-
thers the argument that Jerusalem was a major cultic center in
pre-Hebrew times.

Even prior to David's capture of Jerusalem, there may have
been early contacts between the city and the nation of Israel.
Genesis 14, however late it was rewritten, surely contains some
ancient memories. Melchizedek brings forth bread and wine.

While it has been disputed that his bread and wine constituted a sacrifice (some scholars feared that this was an anachronism, clear only to the poetic eyes of the Christian Fathers), the Ugaritic material makes clear that bread and wine are the stuff of cult. Melchizedek is identified as the priest of *Salem* which at least once in the Old Testament is identified with Zion (*Ps.* 76:3). The identification of the two is clearer from inner criteria —the theology presented—than from any "harder" evidence.

Jerusalem and Creation

Genesis 14 carries references to *El Elyon*, "the highest El," who is maker of Heaven and Earth. Stolz uses this phrase as an argument for the antiquity of the entire passage, since Hebrew interest in the reflective study of creation comes late. Moreover, the word order "heaven and earth" is specifically Mesopotamian. "Earth and heaven" is the more usual word order when Northwest Semitic sources talk of creation. Largely for this reason, Stolz sees here "an erratic block of Jebusite piety" left standing in the text of Genesis. Only here in the entire Old Testament is *Elyon* used as an adjective; otherwise it is a noun. This passage leaves no doubt that the scriptures are talking about El the Creator and giving him a title; they are not talking about any *Elyon* whom the heathens may worship. So was this block of Jebusite theology made inoffensive to pious ears.

A Pre-Hebraic Psalm?

A detailed study of some of the psalms reveals the sort of theological transition which took place in Jerusalem. A classical example is Psalm 29, describing the transition from Canaanite to Hebrew worship. The psalm is an extended metaphor of the power which belongs to a god who rules storms. His voice is on the waters; he thunders over many waters (verse 2). The "many waters" is a Hebrew idiom corresponding to cosmic waters, the waters of chaos. References abound to lightning. The voice of the Lord makes hinds writhe and strips (*wayyehesop*) the forests. (The first reference then is to thunder; the second to lightning.) References to *kavodh* are frequent in the psalms (verses 1, 2, 9). While *kavodh* comes to have all sorts of theological meanings, its first imposition (as in the Greek *doxa*) bears the freight of light imagery (or lightning). The god sits enthroned from the primeval flood over the cosmic waters of chaos (verse 10). That he "sits enthroned as a king" is probably clear enough in the Hebrew *yšb*, but lest we lose the point, the poet says in the second colon, "the god sits as king forever."

The reader should pause now and read the psalm in almost any translation. Some of the above theories may be disputed, but any good English translation should give the flavor of most of it. What is most interesting to us is a phrase in the first verse, where the *bene elim* are called on to yield the right of thunder and lightning to another god. (In the Hebrew version which we have, the "other god" is JHWH. His name shows up frequently. In fact, one might wonder if on a comparative basis the name JHWH shows up more anywhere else than it does in this psalm.)

Bene elim is variously translated. A fairly plausible reading of this would be "sons of El," "adherents of El." The entire psalm can be plausibly read as an effort to get the adherents of El to yield the rights of thunder and lightning to another god. There is a certain historical plausibility to this. Outside of Jerusalem the god of thunder and lightning was Baal-Hadad— not El. All that was required for the use of this psalm in the Hebrew cult was the substitution of the name JHWH for the earlier god. Possibly the pious imprecation of the last verse was added by a later editor: After all this discussion of thunder, lightning, and victories over chaos, the prayer asked that the people will be given peace without which victory is not worth much. The phrase "Lebanon and Sirion" (in verse 6) occurs in a Babylonian fragment of the Gilgamesh epic and in some Ugaritic material.

Some may be puzzled or distressed that we insist we are

dealing with traces of Indo-European (Hittite is Indo-European), Babylonian, and Canaanite materials—all of which flowed into mainstream Old Testament thought. The puzzlement or distress rises largely from a failure to grasp the universality of the "priest-guilds" in the ancient world. Their boundary-free status enabled them to move from region to region—and their ideas moved with them. Today we would hesitate at the easy integration of Buddhist religious practice into mainstream Roman Catholicism. Whether this is better or worse is not the question. We must remind ourselves constantly that the religious world of the ancient Near East was surely different!

It might be useful at this juncture simply to give a translation of Psalm 29. The Hebrew in the psalm is not simple but open to dispute. Still, the following version could be defended as reasonably accurate, if not fine poetry:

A Song of the Reigning King

1. O Sons of El yield to JHWH, yield him *kavodh* and strength.
2. Yield to JHWH. His name is *kavodh*. Bow down at his holy appearance.
3. The voice of JHWH is on the waters. The god of *kavodh* thunders. JHWH is over the cosmic waters.
4. The voice of JHWH is strength and majesty.
5. The voice of JHWH breaks the cedars; yes, JHWH shatters the cedars of Lebanon.
6. He makes them skip like a calf, Lebanon and Sirion like a young bull.
7. The voice of JHWH divides flames of fire.
8. The voice of JHWH shakes the wilderness, JHWH shakes the wilderness of Kadesh.
9. The voice of JHWH makes hinds tremble; (lightning) strips the forests.
10. JHWH is enthroned from the flood, yes, he sits as King forever.
11. May JHWH give strength to his people, May JHWH bless his people with peace.

Much of the psalm is already discussed. Little effort has been made to wrest the translation into a given direction. (The understanding of *hdr* in verse 2 as "theophany" is contained in Stolz's translation of a difficult word.)

What does leap off the page is the repetition of JHWH; this is truly extraordinary. At least one explanation would be that the rewriter had his orthodoxy to prove. Only with that proved, could his poetic re-creation be considered good enough for Jerusalem temple worship.

The City of Peace

For the Christian, of course, Jerusalem has become largely the city of the Christ. Christians largely ignore the fact that Jesus of Nazareth was a pious Jew. Nonetheless, the various gospels bear witness to his life in Jerusalem, his pilgrimages to the city from an early age, his witness and teaching in the Temple precincts, his premonitions of the great distress which would come on the city he loved. To read the gospels even casually as written catechesis is to read of teaching that was often given against the backdrop of what was already then a most ancient religious center.

It remains one of the ironies of history that this city of peace has been the occasion of so much conflict. At least three religious versions put peace at the center of Jerusalem's history (prescinding from the relationship between the *šlm* root and the common Semitic word for peace itself). David took the city, so legend has it, in a "peaceful" manner. So did the Caliph Omar. Jesus of Nazareth, the gospels recall, walked its streets and preached a religion of pacifism. And wars have swirled around the city through all this.

> Ten measures of beauty gave God to the world; nine to Jerusalem and one to all the rest.
> Ten measures of sorrow gave God to the world; one to the world beyond her walls, but nine to Jerusalem.

So goes the Jewish saying. Does God somehow will the

sadness that is in Jerusalem and which is allied to her beauty?
Is this a strident thought? It need not be. To attain his ends
the Divinity can use even sorrows which rise from human evil.

Will it ever be possible to attain the goal of harmony among
those who dwell in Jerusalem? One would think so. Three religions insist that it is the City of Peace, having several times
been "captured" by peaceful methods. In historical fact, an
enormous amount of religious dialogue has gone on in this city.
Jebusites inherited an international religious tradition, mediated perhaps through Ugarit. Hebrews dialogued with Jebusites.
Christianity flowed from a dialogue with Jews. The Muslim
self-image sees itself as sharing the best of Christianity and
Judaism. It should not be impossible for the Divinity to attain
his ends in Jerusalem, to attain a measure of harmony among
those who love him.

But his ends may be a long time coming. When they do
come, three religions believe that Jerusalem will once again
play her proper role as God's dwelling place and the home of
men who are at peace.

God is our Lord and your Lord.
We have our deeds and you have your deeds;
There is no argument between us and you.
God shall bring us together, and His is the homecoming.

Koran, Sura 42

And seeing the city he wept and said, "Jerusalem!
That you might learn the lessons that lead toward peace!"

Lk. 19:41-2

Pray for peace in Jerusalem.

Ps. 122:6

10
Athletes of God

It is a common and justified complaint among modern Jews that Christians misunderstand the Old Testament. (We already cited their complaint about the use of the term "Old Testament" and our attempts to justify the use of it.) Basically, Jews feel that many Christians think of the Old Testament as something that has significance only in terms of Christianity. It is hoped that we have put that idea to rout for some Christians. At least occasionally in this book we have adverted to the liveliness of contemporary Jewish religious thought and the long post-biblical tradition which undergirds that strength.

But at times the scholar, attempting to put his own religious prejudices to one side, may wonder if some contemporary Jews make mistakes in reading the Old Testament that are at least analogous to those made by the Christians whom they (and we) criticize. Do modern Jews sometimes underestimate the vibrant complexity that lies in the Hebrew scriptures? They might if they read the Old Testament exclusively in terms of their own religious practice. Each contemporary Jewish community lives a *stratum* of the Old Testament thought, developed and enriched, surely, by many other sources. But even as they have added much to the stratum which they have lived out, so they have ignored many other Old Testament strata. (This is not a criticism of modern Jews. It is equally applicable to modern Christians, but almost everybody knows that.) In other words, this chapter contends that the modern *qahal* which is the Jewish community has read the Old Testament in a creative fashion that is different from the creative manner in which it has been read by the modern Christian community. The dialogue between book and communities goes on.

At least the implications of this chapter will be that certain selected areas of the Old Testament have enormous significance for contemporary Jewish practice, and a suggestion is here made that perhaps some contemporary Jews do not sufficiently appreciate the fact. (It is hoped that this is more than the medieval *lis de verbis* [struggle over words], but a real difference of opinion.) Mine may be a courageous thesis for an Irish Catholic to proffer, but then without courage one does not write books.

Let us put our difference of opinion this way: We contend that the contemporary Jewish world sees itself as non-ascetic in atmosphere. But in our judgment contemporary Judaism is ascetic, and the asceticism flows from dynamics which were operative in the Hebrew scriptures. As proof for the Jewish self-view as non-ascetic, consider the presentation given in Rabbi Gordis' little book *Conservative Judaism* published by the United Synagogues of America.

Let me offer a personal definition of asceticism: it is "the voluntary seeking of the difficult or painful out of love for the Divinity." So understood, asceticism, we feel, is found throughout Judaism.

In the history of many religious traditions, asceticism has served at least three functions. Listing them in ascending order of value (judged subjectively), we note that ascetic practices have served as punishment, as training, and as externalization. The first use is simply described. The devout judges that he has transgressed in one area or other. No action on earth will make the transgression a non-thing. It happened. It is. So he voluntarily takes on himself a difficult or painful action because it is a substitute (albeit a poor substitute) for being able to blot out the action by which he has offended the Divinity.

Secondly, the devout sees himself as an athlete in training. He does not know when the next challenge will come on him. He does not know the nature of the next challenge. But he feels that he must be stronger than he now is. He judges that "spiritual strength" or "strength of will" can be increased through practice, as muscles grow through exercise, as the thinking process grows through constant thought, as the creative process grows through creative reflection. So he trains by denying himself a good, here and now, that he may resist an evil in the hidden future.

If some persons (ascetics and non-ascetics) are unsympathetic with the first two descriptions, perhaps the next aspect of asceticism may seem a bit more tolerable. Asceticism derives from a need to externalize. The devout, as any lover, has a need to show his love. The fact that the Divinity needs nothing which the lover has to offer, slows him down only slightly. He has a need to show something, and so he turns to asceticism, voluntary seeking of difficult or painful things, precisely because they allow him to externalize without deluding himself into thinking that he is filling a hidden need of the Divinity.

The question here is one of emphasis. If that third aspect of asceticism is valid (and some would judge it to be the best of asceticism) then the following is at least of interest. The world of the Old Testament was much concerned with externalization of love for the Divinity. The ordinary way that this took place during most of the Old Testament period was through cultic sacrifice.

This practice ought not to be seen as monolithic. The rather simple outdoor sacrifice of the patriarchal period is not to be confused with the stylized ritual of the temple. But at one point a certain mode of externalization—temple sacrifice—became accepted as virtually the only mode. At this juncture the sacredness of Zion was established; it was identified as the dwelling place of JHWH and the idea gained acceptance that Zion would never fall. Zion then did fall, and the resulting theological crisis led to one of history's great theological leaps forward.

During the exile the learned among the Hebrews sought a form of externalization that could supplant the no longer existing temple cult. Exposed in Babylon to an intellectual milieu superior perhaps to anything they had yet seen, the more learned Hebrews moved toward substituting *law* for cult. But this required asceticism on at least two levels. First, it required asceticism for the scholars themselves; they sacrificed lifetimes of hard work in order to be able to point out the detailed will of JHWH in fuller measure. (Do not commit *reṣah*! When is it *reṣah* and when is it not? What circumstances permit the taking of human life? What constitutes human life?) Secondly, there was the asceticism required to observe the minutiae of the law. The prohibition, "Do not boil a kid in its mother's milk" (*Ex.* 23:19), began as a reaction against a pagan custom. It grew into a requirement prohibiting meat and milk at the same meal, requiring different sets of dishes, and enforcing the complexities of *kashrut,* the stern but beautiful dietary laws which in so many ages have distinguished Jews from non-Jews and encouraged Jews to socialize only with Jews, keeping intermarriage with gentiles down to a minimum.

So powerful did these legal dynamics become that with the return after the exile it was impossible to eliminate them and go back to simple cultic observance. The manner of externalization through law had a religious charm all its own.

One of the beauties of this asceticism in the Old Testament was that it worked in opposition to another valuable dynamic which, if unchecked, would have done great harm to what was to become modern Judaism. In the chapter on Deuteronomy we noted the advantages of centralized worship and the unified priestly caste living in Jerusalem. As a corollary, though, this meant the death of small, local shrines and the rural priesthood. Because of this development some scholars (notably the Israeli Weinfeld) see Deuteronomy as a *secularizing* force. The small shrines encouraged the notion that religion was something which belonged to the whole of life. Centralization of worship worked against that notion. In fact, it ran the risk of strengthening the idea that religion was something that was practiced only in a special place. But the asceticism which the law required turned all this around again. Laws which were to be observed in the kitchen and by the hearth, in bathroom and barn, reestablished once and for all the idea that religion was something that permeated all human existence. In this is Judaism blessed (and has blessed her daughters, Christianity and Islam). Even those areas of Jewish practice today which do not accept the complexities of later Jewish law cling fast to the notion that religion cannot be separated from any areas of human existence.

The reader might be advised to pause here and study some

of the legal selections given at the back of the book and the "Holiness Code" of Leviticus 17-26 and to reflect on them. Sometimes one hears it said (in almost any religious group): "This is not the church (or synagogue or religious order) I joined!" Perhaps the discouragement in that exclamation is occasionally justified. One wonders, though, if sometimes such a remark is not as sensible as the outcry of anguished parents who look at their seven-foot teenager and lament, "This is not the six-pound baby we brought home from the hospital." Indeed he is not. Living things grow.

Much that is best in contemporary Jewish practice seems, to the outsider, to be derived from that living dynamic when law becomes a valid substitute for cult. Law became a means to externalize love for JHWH. And, to one observer, this is what asceticism is all about.

The role of the rabbi developed, at least *in germine*, from this juncture. The previously combined teaching and blessing-sacrificial functions became now irrevocably separated. The caste which was to become the professional rabbi took to itself (or was given perhaps by the community) the role of instructing the young. With the passage of time an opposition grew up between rabbi and priest. This obscured the fact that the rabbinate may well have been Levitical in terms of its ultimate origin.

It is almost impossible to exaggerate the complexity involved in the origins of the Hebrew-Judaic legal system. Certainly the exposure to the Babylonian legal system gave a new impetus to the Hebrews' love of law. The non-availability of a suitable temple in Babylon was another impetus. But throughout this book we have alluded to the existence of a kind of judgment-cult, reaching back almost to patriarchal times. This cult began a dynamic whose power reaches to the present day. Originally it was found in a liturgical setting where disputes between one Hebrew and another were decided and enforced. We have suggested that this cult gave rise eventually to a code of law.

But no law code can be applied automatically. In order to apply the laws properly a disciplined system of study was

created. Largely from this study grew the separate profession of
the rabbinate which lives with us (to the enormous profit of the
Hebrew people) until the present day. And Jewish asceticism is
most beautifully exercised precisely by that rabbinate.

Problems of Wisdom

Long prior to the rise of the rabbinate, the same ascetical
milieu made possible the rise of the wisdom literature. An excellent description of the joys that wisdom eventually offers is
given by T. H. White in his classic, *The Once and Future
King.* The wizard Merlyn delivers an impassioned description
of those joys, saying:

> The best thing for being sad . . . is to learn something.
> That is the only thing that never fails. You may grow old
> and trembling in your anatomies, you may lie awake at
> night listening to the disorder of your veins, you may miss
> your only love, you may see the world about you devastat-
> ed by evil lunatics, or know your honour trampled in the
> sewers of baser minds. There is only one thing for it then—
> to learn. Learn why the world wags and what wags it. That
> is the only thing which the mind can never exhaust, never
> alienate, never be tortured by, never fear or distrust, and
> never dream of regretting. Learning is the thing for you.
> Look at what a lot of things there are to learn—pure
> science, the only purity there is. You can learn astronomy
> in a lifetime, natural history in three, literature in six. And
> then, after you have exhausted a milliard lifetimes in biol-
> ogy and medicine and theocriticism and geography and
> history and economics—why, you can start to make a cart-
> wheel out of the appropriate wood, or spend fifty years
> learning to begin to learn to beat your adversary at fenc-
> ing. After that you can start again on mathematics, until
> it is time to learn to plough.

Merlyn's eloquence is a fine description of the world of wisdom which the Hebrews inherited. But finding sacredness in wisdom presents problems. In fact, one of the difficulties of the wisdom literature for the student of the Hebrew scriptures is the manner in which these books got included in the Canon—the list of approved (even required) sacred readings. The answer is not impossibly difficult from one viewpoint. After the Hebrew world decided that wisdom was a gift of God, then to know was to know God. But coming to realize that wisdom must be sacred, since to know is to know God, was not easy. For the world around Israel which produced the wisdom milieu, the atmosphere out of which these books grew, was largely non-God if not anti-God in orientation.

Scholars have vigorously disputed among themselves how the books of wisdom became accepted finally. (Basically, we are talking here about Proverbs, Ecclesiastes, Job, Ben Sira, and the Wisdom of Solomon.) Explanations vary. None of them is totally satisfactory. Similarly, explanations vary in attempting to show how these books originated in the first place. Efforts have been made in recent years to trace them back to some kind of liturgical setting. Other scholars see them as originating from an international "intellectuals' guild" which existed in close conjunction with the cult. (Remember the evidence which has already been presented in the book for a kind of international caste of religious personnel?) An argument for this view is that writings are found in languages other than Hebrew which seem much to correspond with the sort of thing that a given Hebrew book is trying to do. *Ludlul Bel Nemeqi*, "I praise the lord of wisdom," struggles with the problems of suffering and the just man. *Ahikar*, a wise man, tries to show through pithy expressions a type of wisdom for all occasions, much like Proverbs. (*Ahikar* is mentioned in the book of Tobit, accepted by Roman Catholics as canonical wisdom but generally not so accepted by Jews and non-Catholic Christians.)

The wisdom literature is strange and different. It does not seem to be in contact with the world which most of us know. "The Lord does not let the righteous go hungry" (*Prov.* 10:3), for example, is not true to the experience most of us have had. We see that some righteous men prosper and many do not.

Where did this "wisdom" come from? Some scholars feel from such verses and from the generally self-satisfied tone of the works (Job would be a notable exception) that wisdom literature originated in the world of the bureaucratic scholar. This was a generally happy and self-controlled world. Such a scholar could guarantee himself a degree of prosperity. Then in his middle or late years he had the time and leisure to tell younger men "how it was all done." If one is wise in his dealings with women (*Prov.* 6:24-29 and *Prov.* 19:14), firm in dealings with his children (*Prov.* 19:18), discreet in dealings with his superior (*Prov.* 15:5), life will continue to get better. The examples could be multiplied many times. Suffice it to say that the general tone of much of the wisdom literature is a fairly self-satisfied older and wiser man giving solemn and sleepy instruction to the young who are not terribly eager to listen. This is not a terribly attractive portrait. It is also not totally accurate. It does not describe all of the wisdom literature all of the time. But it does describe a substantial stratum of it. For this reason, we may ask again the question, "How did this become successfully integrated into the mainstream of Hebrew literature and canonized as worthy and required reading?"

Where We Differ

Anthropologist Margaret Mead classifies societies (among other ways) as pre-figurative, con-figurative, or post-figurative. The criterion for these different categories is whether the bulk of a given population's individuals put most emphasis on citizens who preceded them in life, their peer-group, or the generation which is yet to come.

At the time when she first presented these classifications, she noted that American society was on its way to becoming post-figurative, since the models most influencing significant people in America were not so much the younger generation as the generation yet unborn. She wrote that significant decisions were being made in light of the mood (not really the intellectual thought processes) which we thought would be characteristic of the generation yet unborn. A puzzling business.

The Hebrew world would find incomprehensible the idea that a younger generation should be taken as a norm of decision-making. Wisdom is something that comes with age. It is partially for this reason that age is honored. Age is the repository of a national treasure. It is easy to criticize this notion in a technological age. The "wisdom" of a hundred years ago seems useless to us in terms of all that has happened in the world of science and machines since then. Oddly enough, some believe that there was a feeling for this argument in the world of the Old Testament. Wisdom among the elderly is treasured not because it is useful for today or tomorrow; rather, there may be a more distant future where a generation yet unborn may have need of that wisdom. Such wisdom will not exist if we do not treasure it now.

Whether one agrees or disagrees with those feelings is beside the point. It may be in light of the above feelings that the Hebrew world found much of the wisdom literature congenial. Much of the wisdom material is not sufficiently heedful of God; much of it seems to be at least gently cynical in its advice on "how to get ahead" in this world. Still, it is basically concerned with the wisdom of the aged and the experienced and is much preoccupied with transmitting that wisdom and the effects of that experience to a younger, inexperienced, and less wise generation. No world has ever loved the coming generation more than the worlds of Hebrew and Jew. Perhaps if for no other reason they found the preoccupations of the wisdom literature to be something from God.

Moreover, while most of the wisdom literature is late, it is not without earlier adumbrations and a consequent ring of authority. The book of Samuel gives us a good description of the role which Ahithophel played in the entourage of David: "And the counsel of Ahithophel who gave advice in those days was significant. It was as though one had inquired of an oracle from God" (2 *Sam.* 16:23). This man shows up some fifteen or twenty times by name in the book of Samuel. He is given an official ranking by the later historical work Chronicles (1 *Chron.* 27:33); this same work gives him either an assistant or a successor (1 *Chron.* 27:34); the Hebrew is ambiguous. In any event, the role of professional "wise man" has antecedents that reach far, far back into Hebrew history. In addition, scholars who do not hold generally for "oral composition" are frequently willing to see some of the wisdom literature to be a faithful written rendition of material with deep oral antecedents. Briefly put then, Israel "felt comfortable" with the wisdom literature as with something ancient. The kinds of incompatibility which some of us moderns see between this literature and the patriarchal narratives or the eloquence of the prophets just did not bother them.

There is one further unifying dimension to the asceticism (athleticism) which we have looked at in the development of *legalism* and *wisdom*. It was the belief that the whole of life belonged to God. We are talking about human life. Therefore, if human sexuality has a proper place in the Hebrew scriptures —and it most assuredly does—then those exhilarating moments which are intellectual in origin and which belong only to humans must have their place also. Some of the wisdom literature—the simplistic proverbs, for example—may leave us with a feeling that part of the Hebrew world underestimated the powers of intellect. But surely the book of Job and some of the more tender observations of Ecclesiastes, "the race is not always to the swift . . ." (*Eccles.* 9:11), give us another side of the human capacity to reflect if not always to know. If to know is to know God, then to strive to know is to strive to know God.

The wisdom literature is occasionally pompous. But even at its most pompous, it has one preoccupation which is tender. It sees life correctly as a race between physical deterioration and the acquisition of maturity. The relatively wise man knows both that he is wise and that he is only relatively wise. He sees also that his physical—and perhaps his psychological—powers are failing him. And so he reaches out to the young. He knows (since after all he is wise) that he cannot place old heads on young shoulders, but he would hope that at least some of his mistakes need not be made all over again, that what he has learned from them may be handed on to the young. And if he happens to sound a trifle opinionated in the process of handing on, who can remain angry with him?

Occasionally a flash of humor relieves his heaviness, "Like a gold ring in a pig's nose is beauty in a woman without common sense" (*Prov.* 11:22). Occasionally he forgets his own wise observation that he is not the source of his own wisdom, "Let not the wise man glory in his wisdom; rather let him glory that he knows me" (*Jer.* 9:23-24). Generally, though, he understands the source of his wisdom as ancient Israel did, "And all Israel rejoiced at the wisdom which God had given him" (1 *Kings* 3:28).

And if he occasionally forgets this and sounds just a trifle pompous, he is quickly forgiven by the reader. Pomposity is easily forgiven when it asserts itself in a beloved great-grandfather who really only wishes to teach and to help.

A Dialogic Postscript

Most of the chapters in this book have been read by colleagues and students with resultant discussion. Some chapters have been considerably shaped by that discussion. Perhaps no portion has received sharper reaction from the kindly circle that has helped the author than the section of the preceding chapter which dealt most directly with asceticism.

The chapter could not be rewritten on the basis of that advice for reasons which will become clear. Simply put, the objections raised were not precisely with the conclusions which the chapter offered but with the modus. Some wondered if the word "asceticism" ought to be used at all in a book written for a Jewish as well as a Christian audience. In what follows, the author will try to sum up the reactions of some earlier readers.

It is interesting to the Protestant to realize that there is fairly widespread feeling against "Puritanism" among Catholics of a certain age and a certain level of education. This is interesting to the Protestant—of almost any tradition—because "Puritanism" seems really to represent an "asceticism" that is quite analogous to the Roman Catholic monastic tradition. This latter speaks of poverty, chastity, and obedience. And so, in other words, did the Puri-

tans and some contemporary Protestant traditions which
are derivative. "Poverty" becomes stewardship of money,
time, property and learning. "Chastity" becomes the rules
that govern family and marriage. "Obedience," mediated
by one's peers, is owed by all to God.

Can it be that asceticism takes many forms and that
frequently the practitioner of one form does not often ad-
vert to his life-style as "ascetic"? That the most ascetic
among Protestants or Catholics is basically a happy and
fulfilled person? Consequently, he tends to dwell on the
satisfaction that his religion offers him and to be quick to
see negative aspects of asceticism only in other forms of
religious practice.

But in speaking with Jews there is a further problem in
the use of the term "ascetic." In fact, one may wonder if
the term is beyond redemption. Yet, as the word is used,
theoretically, it does describe wide ranging aspects of contemporary Jewish life and practice. Still, the Jewish world
might reasonably object to it. Historically and philologi-
cally the term can be salvaged. But does it carry too great
a burden of emotional freight?

For many persons, not only Jews, the term "asceticism"
hints at a kind of dualism, a suggestion that there is a
wedge between God and his creation. This is not without
foundation. What does the Christian scholar mean when
he speaks of "eschatological humanism"? How long can
one talk about a humanism that is colored by the *eschata*
without touching close on dualism? For those who see "asceticism" in Christianity as derivative from a preoccupation with the End of Days, the term bears such emotional
burdens as to be utterly useless in talking about Judaism.

For most Jews, the dichotomy between the secular and
the sacred does not exist. This world does not have somehow to be "sacramentalised"; it is already holy. Wherever
the Jew takes hold of life, he finds the Divinity already at
work.

And here the postscript ends with no resolution. Language
has its limits, and perhaps dialogue among religions stretches

them. Readers agreed that while the term "asceticism" was poor, in their judgment, the definition which we offered, "The voluntary seeking of the painful out of love for the Divinity," would perhaps be acceptable to a Jewish audience. But, someone noted, the average Jew might well feel that "common seeking of the painful" was an uncommon necessity for him. It comes on him without the search.

And so the dialogue continues between the Old Testament and a variety of communities, and among those communities. These dialogues, it is hoped, will bring us ever closer to one goal seldom found in this life—unchanging truth.

11

Sacral Kingship

This chapter and the two that follow deal with the manner in which the *qahal* of New Testament times (the *ecclesia*) came to grips with three specific themes from the Hebrew scriptures. The believing Christian may find something in these chapters that will illuminate and deepen his knowledge of the New Testament. The believing Jew will presumably disagree with the use that the New Testament has made of the three themes of sacral kingship, the servant of God, and the prophet. He will nonetheless find the study of these themes as they occur in the Old Testament to be of great interest. Moreover, as he examines the reasons why the New Testament came to use these themes at all, he will probably have a variety of reactions. First, he will be flattered and surprised at the influence that the Old Testament has had on the most central themes of Christian preaching. Secondly, he may be puzzled at learning how Jewish the New Testament is, and wonder, if this be the case, why there has been so much antipathy between Jew and Christian over the centuries. There is no ready answer. Perhaps one can only say that such quarrels have been family quarrels, and religious family quarrels at that. These are the sharpest of all human conflicts.

The believing and intellectual Christian with some knowledge of the Old Testament will have his own set of problems with these chapters. An earlier age saw the Old Testament as a rather simple collection of "clues" pointing to the coming Messiah. For that age, all the goodhearted person had to do was to read the Old Testament faithfully, discern the clues, and then recognize Jesus of Nazareth as the promised one. Such simplicity was wrong on a number of counts. Among other things it ignored the central Christian teaching on the "gratuity of grace," the "wind that blows where it will" (*Jn.* 3:8), calling one man to the Father via one route, calling one man by another. From this doctrine we can see it is impossible that there could be anything so automatic as the reading of books, the discerning of clues, and then immediate access to the Father through the Christ.

And there are other difficulties with the simplist view. Some references to the Christ that was to come may in hindsight look quite clear to some of us. (Ronald Knox used to delight in pointing out that Christians feel that they read the Old Testament now the way ancient Greek audiences followed their drama. They came to the theater knowing how it was going to turn out.) But those references read without Christian hindsight are not clear. In fact, the early Christians did not so read the Old Testament. Rather, reflecting on their own faith experience with Christ, they strove in the preaching that was to become the New Testament, to describe that experience in terms of the best-loved religious literature at their disposal: the Old Testament—the only texts that they believed to be "sacred scripture," the only religious literature which Jesus of Nazareth, we may presume, studied and learned to love from earliest years.

In this chapter and the two that follow we will maintain that at least three Old Testament themes (and assuredly others) are woven through the New Testament in reference to the Christ whom the New Testament church experienced: these themes are sacral kingship, the servant of God, and the prophet.

One aspect of the thesis is a bold one; perhaps it is most open to challenge in the matter of sacral kingship. How much did the people of the New Testament era know of sacral kingship? For these chapters to have any real validity, an insight of Professor James Barr in the area of linguistics may be of some use. The insight is fairly simple in the context in which he used it, but it may have far wider implications than he realized. The insight was this: Professor Barr felt that reading texts *later* than the text under study was often more useful in understanding troublesome passages than the generally accepted procedure of reading passages earlier in time. His reasoning was that the written material of a given era only captures a small amount of the living language of that time. A troublesome passage, let us say, from the year 1000 B.C. might easily be explained by a passage from the year 200 B.C. The crucial word, found in a broad context in the earlier passage, might be found in a more precisely defined context in the later text. It could still be the same usage because it had lived in the language for some eight hundred years and *had only occasionally been written down.*

Perhaps a contemporary example may help. (It is not easy to find good contemporary examples. Much language usage today has the life-span of the black-bellied fruit fly, but let us attempt.) If a college student writing a formal letter in the early 1970's were to slip in formal diction and to use the expressions "cool" or "groovy," his biographers in the year 2070 might be puzzled. Consulting the dictionaries of formal language they would find that "cool" meant the absence of heat and that "groovy" meant to be equipped with ridges and hollows. The mode in which the student used the expressions does not normally occur in formal written speech. But then, one of his biographers discovers in the year 2000 a written account of a conversation with careful context making clear the meaning of the word. That this could happen is due to the fact that even in highly literate societies (and the ancient Near East was not such) *language usage is far broader outside the written page than on it.*

The point being made here goes farther than Barr's original insight. If we want to come to terms with the theological meaning of sacral kingship in the world of, let us say, King David, we may profitably explore notions of sacral kingship found long before or long after King David. For the printed page is far more narrow than the living theology which flows around it. It may even be that the idea of sacral kingship continued to flourish in the common Hebrew psyche of New Testament times—although its exercise was no longer a practical reality— and that the Church taught not precisely from the ideas of the written Old Testament pages but from those ideas as they were understood by the commentary written on the fleshly tablets of the contemporary Jewish heart (2 *Cor.* 3:3). But perhaps we have already gone too far without answering the question: What is sacral kingship?

Sacral Kingship

It is a commonplace to observe in Old Testament scholarship that the world of the Old Testament views all kingship in the light of the king that David was. If the messiah, for example, is ever presented as a king, he is a king on the model of David. Perhaps so idealized did David become to the Hebrew mind that it was hard to imagine anything much better. Still, in the Old Testament world that existed long before David there was a motif of the majesty of royalty. This motif continued to resound in Old Testament writings long after David.

For example, in Lamentations 4:20 we read: "The breath of our nostrils, the anointed of the Lord, was taken in their pits, of whom we said: 'Under his shadow we shall live among the heathen.'" The passage, whatever its meaning, is post-exilic, written far after the time of David. But it brings to mind an Akkadian passage, descriptive of the role of the king as the Babylonian-Assyrian world viewed it. "Men are the shadow of God, but the King is God's image!" The playing with words is complicated and perhaps not totally clear by Western standards, but it is not impossible to see in the refrain of Lamentations the notion that men could have hoped to live under the shadow of the king who was himself the image of God.

If the above suggestion is correct, it would be but one more imitation of a theological dynamic often operative in the world of the Old Testament. Long prior to historic events in Hebrew history, there existed powerful mythic realities. Here it was the notion of the king as God's image where men are only God's shadow. Then an historical event takes place. Later generations, in efforts to communicate to their young the majesty of that event's effect, tend to indulge in "literary heightening." Sometime after this is done, the common psyche of the people hearkens back to the myth, sees the relationship between the myth and the now-heightened reality and the two somewhat fuse.

Let us take a clearer example. Why is the king sacred? In the world of myth, the Divinity frequently has to conquer what is to become his sacred mountain. In the history of David's own life, the city of Jerusalem and its "impregnable" fortress fall to him by ruse of some sort and without apparently much loss of life—a remarkable feature in any war but certainly in a war of the ancient Near East. This factual foundation, that David (or his lieutenants) took the citadel without much loss of life becomes exaggerated in time. This "exaggeration" is faithful to reality. It is only an effort to communicate to the younger generation that did not experience the emotional impact of the factual peaceful conquest the enormous emotional relief that it meant to those actually involved. In the mythic antecedents to this event, there is a powerful motif of the conquest of the sacred mountain by the Divinity. The deity, in a variety of ancient Near Eastern religions, must conquer the mountain which is to become his powerful dwelling place, the cosmic site that corresponds to the sanctuary of his temple. This is part of the theme of the Divine Warrior. To those actually involved in David's conquest of Jerusalem the connection between the factual event and this one aspect of the Divine Warrior was not clear. However, with the passage of time and with the literary heightening of the event, the correspondence seemed to be a very real one. To those who shared a deep insight into the emotional effect of the conquest, the parallel between David's conquest and the momentous victory of the deity in pre-history seemed quite clear. What is the nature of sacral kingship in the Old Testament? Does it contain traces of "divine kingship" in which the king is truly god? It is possible, and some fine scholars have defended the idea. It is extremely difficult to prove, however. Perhaps it is more sound to say that sacral kingship in the Old Testament is a blending or conflation of two ideas. One of them may be that the king himself is divine—a common notion in the ancient Near East. The second is that the king is an ideal human. The resulting blend—sacral kingship— asserts that the king is most holy in a very special manner because of his unique relationship to the great Divinity.

One place where there is some evidence of this confusion is in Psalm 132 in its present form. David is praised for his work in finding a dwelling place for the Divinity (verses 3-5), and yet the Divinity himself has chosen the dwelling place (verses 13-14). Moreover, there is a clearer reference to the Divinity as warrior himself. "Arise O Lord from thy rest, thou and the ark of thy strength!" (verse 8) This is a reference to the Divine Warrior who fights for Israel. We find references in the Old Testament to the bringing of the ark of the covenant onto the field of battle. The *teruah* (sacred battle cry) is shouted. It seems at times that the Divinity is actually encouraged to "rise" from the ark and to scatter his enemies. When the enemies are scattered, he may rest as do the fighting men of Israel (cf. *Num.* 10:34-36). It is interesting to note the Hebrew construction in Psalm 132:8 *limnuhateka*. In older Hebrew (and in Ugaritic) the initial *l* means "from." In later Hebrew, it generally means "to." Not only does the translation "from" make more sense here, but it enables us to date this verse back toward an era which would be more at ease with the notion of the Divine Warrior who "rises from his rest" to fight for Israel and "returns" to it only when victory is achieved.

There is an interesting example in this psalm of the mode in which the Hebrew mind operates. Its logic is neither better nor worse than that of the Western mind, but quite different. One idea reminds the Hebrew of another. The causality by which one idea flows from another is real, but somewhat difficult to reproduce in a syllogism. Consider Psalm 132 for example. The Divinity is the warrior who chooses his own dwelling, and he presumably conquers it as in Canaanite mythology. David, historically a warrior, is viewed here rather as the "keeper of the ark" and is for that reason himself "sacral." But the ark is the place from which the divine warrior arises in times of conflict and to which he returns in times of repose. And so these ideas all flow together: The historical David who is a warrior, the Divinity who is warrior at least in myth, the conquest of the cosmic mountain, the taking of the real citadel of Jerusalem in mysterious fashion (2 *Sam.* 5:6-9). Lastly, in this relationship of David to the ark there is a fairly simple dimension of "sacral kingship" in the Old Testament. The king is "holy" since he takes care of holy things: David the ark, Solomon the temple, and Josiah the long process of reformation.

Patternism and Sacral Kingship

Briefly put, this is the theory of "patternism" in Old Testament scholarship. If one is dealing with cultures A and B and C and finds a multitude of demonstrable parallels through all three cultures, one may argue to the existence of other not-easily demonstrated parallels in a third culture if they are clearly present to two of the cultures in question. Nowhere is the usefulness of this mode of argumentation more clear than in dealing with the fuller dimensions of sacral kingship. There is rich, substantial documentation in the Akkadian material for a wide range of ideas swirling around the motif of sacral kingship. These ideas clearly include such elements as humiliation, death, and resurrection of a sacral king. Significant documentation, but by no means so rich, can be found in the Ugaritic material. In the Old Testament material, evidences for the fuller dimensions of the motif are best described as vestigial. But that they are genuine vestiges is indicated by the richness of the ideas in the parallel cultures of Babylonia-Assyria (Akkadian) and the world represented by the Ugaritic material.

Why so? Two of the cultures may be described as "frozen." They developed an idea of a king who was somehow a god and were never much embarrassed by the notion. The third culture continued to grow to the point where it felt that the divine king was not compatible with its monotheism. Caught between the *pietas* dynamic of which we have spoken earlier and the need to be faithful to transmitted traditions, this culture produced textual references which could be read in a variety of ways. And to some of those Old Testament texts we shall eventually turn.

First, mention should be made of the Babylonian *Akitu* festival. Akkadian texts richly document a number of the facets of this religious festival. The festival is a "New Year's ritual." In it the king plays a central role. He makes standard allusions to his role as the Divinity's adoptive son. He makes intercessory prayer for his people. He recognizes himself as the source of justice for his people. He is both the personal embodiment of justice and makes decisions of justice between persons. (1 Kings 3:5 ff. puts many of these thoughts in the mouth of Solomon who is ascending the throne.) The *Akitu* festival was also a festival of "renewal" of the kingship of a given individual, a new beginning.

In certain aspects of the *Akitu* festival, there is confusion of the divinity and the king. On one level, the *Akitu* festival is a celebration of the coming to power by a given king. It is a new year's festival, the celebration of renewal, a beginning again. In some of the texts at our disposal, no matter the name of the reigning king, the people are trained to shout at a climactic moment: "Let Marduk become king!" (Marduk was the chief deity of the time.) What do Marduk and the king precisely have in common? They make decisions. Marduk hands over to the king the possibility of making judgments. The king then makes acts of judgment as a reflection of the activity of the Divinity in a cosmic sphere. (Remember that cult is almost inevitably an acting out of cosmic activity; in this context it is activity that takes place "in Heaven.")

How are these ideas a backdrop of New Testament messianic thought? New Testament references to Christ as king are vague. This is inevitable. The New Testament is concerned with Christ as he is received in faith. Its religious writing is then, of necessity, suggestive and allusive. An example may help. In a contemporary novel, the protagonist is described early in the book as being the most handsome male who ever lived. Or rather he is not described: The statement is simply made that he is such. The author then hastily adds that he will never describe the protagonist. Each of us has his own image of what constitutes human beauty. If the hero is described in any specific way, he will lack a component that one reader seeks, or will have too much of something that another reader feels should be had in small amounts. Either would destroy the image. So the New Testament alludes now to Christ as king, now as servant, now as prophet in veiled language, making possible the penetration of the veil in sundry ways by the human heart and the Divine Spirit.

Another reason for the New Testament to veil its references to Christ the king was its well-founded fear of state authorities. While one could stress that Christ's kingdom was not of this world (*Jn.* 18:36), the distinction might be lost on the state— with direst consequences. Nonetheless, the expressions Kingdom of God, Kingdom of Heaven, and Eternal Kingdom appear approximately two hundred times in the New Testament. In many of the contexts, Christ's unique role in the kingdom does shine through. "Will you at this time restore the Kingdom to Israel?" he is naively asked (*Acts* 1:6). The title is put, derisively in the mouths of his enemies. "He says he is Christ— a King" (*Lk.* 23:2), Pilate's soldiers strike the "King of the Jews" and give him a crown of thorns (*Mk.* 15:16-19, *Jn.* 19:2). He is mocked at his crucifixion: "Let the King of Israel come down from the cross" (*Mk.* 15:32). But the Good Thief asks to be admitted into the kingdom where Christ is to come into power very shortly (*Lk.* 23:42). The symbolism of the entry into Jerusalem points clearly to kingship (*Lk.* 19:38). In Matthew 21:5 and John 12:5 the influence of the Old Testament (*Zech.* 9:9) is clearer. "Rejoice daughter of Sion. See how your king comes to you. A faithful saviour, meek and riding on a donkey." Christ fights off the efforts of the crowds to proclaim him king (*Mk.* 6:45). Here as elsewhere (*Mt.* 20:21) the eager supporters see one view of what it is to be Messiah-King, and Christ sees something else. *Revelation* shows little restraint. Christ is the "ruler of the kings of earth" (*Rev.* 1:5), the "king of kings" (*Rev.* 17:14), the "Lion of the Tribe of Judah" (*Rev.* 5:5), the "root and offspring of David" (*Rev.* 22:16). It should be admitted that these New Testament sources differ among themselves. What they have in common is some access to Old Testament thought and some vision of Christ as king.

What are we to make of the above reflections? In the New Testament all these references may be read now as a hint, now as a suggestion, now as a proclamation for him who has ears to hear. Previously in this chapter we spoke of the fact that the early Christian community wrote the New Testament against the backdrop of oral commentary on the Old Testament. Perhaps the allusion makes more sense now. Texts such as those cited above might not "win a debate" on this issue; still, they do provoke thought.

The sacral king is a pattern against which the Old Testament reflects on what the messiah may be like. He is involved in judgment and the possibility of punishment. He is the center of the cult. (Christ is "sacral king" surely on the cross.) As the priest does in certain Christian denominations which are highly liturgical, the sacral king speaks in the name of the Divinity. Moreover, he is the Divinity's adoptive son. Clearly in the Babylonian material, the sacral king is humiliated, put to death, and "resurrected." Some scholars find evidence for this pattern in the Old Testament, though their findings are vigorously disputed. This much is clear: The pattern of myth, actual event, rehearsed event, and the reinfusion of myth into that later rehearsal occurs again and again in the dynamic of Old Testament composition and editing.

The suggestion that cultic acts involve re-enactment is made, for example, in Psalm 95:7, "O that today you might hear his voice." Historically, the voice has long since spoken, but its words echo. In the liturgy the cultic leader speaks, but the voice of God is heard. Similarly, the ancient victory over "death," actively portrayed in the Ugaritic material, is only hinted at in Psalm 48. God Who is our leader for ever and ever in the battle against death (verse 14). God conquered death in the past; now he is our leader in our own battle against death.

The fact that JHWH battles against Death and triumphs is easily proved throughout the Old Testament. The fact that the triumph is ritually re-enacted and that the ritual re-enactment is done by a sacral king is less easily demonstrated. Still, there are "footprints." Psalm 30, which a later tradition has labelled "A Psalm and Song at the Dedication of the House of David," speaks of the life that has been brought down to the grave and back (verse 3). Weeping endures for the night, but joy comes in the morning (verse 5). Only the most adamant opponents of the death-resurrection motif in the Old Testament could meditate on this psalm for very long and dismiss it without a stray, nagging thought that we have here precisely the reference to the *šar puḫi* of the Babylonian world—the "substitute king" who was actually put to death that the real king might be "resurrected." A more benign version of this simply pretended the death of a king who spent a sleepless night in the temple until joy came in the morning. Finally, Psalm 118 may be easily read as a processional psalm in which the chief interest is centered on the king. He is presented as one who has been chastised and brought to the very gates of "death." Nonetheless, through the power of JHWH, he has been justified.

The notion that a divine king suffers, dies, and is resurrected can be documented in pagan sources with such richness that the documentation may best be left to an appendix. But the fact itself does give rise to a question: Is it "threatening" for the pious Christian to find the ideas of humiliation, death, and resurrection in pagan literatures? Perhaps, but it need not be so. The "threat" comes largely from building a faith on a needlessly simple view of reality. Less faith is required to believe Christian witness to the resurrection of Christ if the idea itself is absolutely unique. But the educated Christian realizes that the early Christians were confronted with a magnificent reality which they came to understand only with the passage of time. We should not retroject our present understanding of that reality back into the earlier age.

But there is another idea why discovering the humiliation, death, and resurrection of a sacral king in pagan literature (and perhaps also in the Old Testament) ought not to frighten Christians. If the Christian theology of creation teaches us anything, it teaches us that the Divinity alone knows what is in the heart of man, as he placed it there. It also teaches that the longing for "redemption"—whatever that may sometimes mean—is a universal longing, and that the mode of redemption may be described in archetypal forms. Man longs to be "redeemed," not by a man totally like himself, but like a person above him—at least a king. The hope that this king should be humiliated, suffer and die as the means of bringing about this redemption—that too may be universal. Humankind knows no deeper witness of love than external testimony through suffering and through the ultimate punishment—death.

The Christian whose faith has been supported by over-simplification and misunderstanding will be bothered by some of the preceding ideas. He might well be encouraged to re-think his faith-stance. But the believing Christian who is intellectual and who therefore accepts challenges to his faith as stimuli to growth may ponder the preceding and conclude: Christianity is deeply human; it reflects values and longings that antedate it. As a Christian, I believe that Christianity is divine in origin. What earlier faith-stances dreamed of in sheer myth, Christianity finds in deep reality cloaked in mythic language.

Hopefully the non-Christian will not find my belief triumphalistic. If his own faith-stance is equally deep, he may well have some analogously comforting feelings of his own. Christians rejoice that he has them, for they acknowledge that the Divinity touches men in different ways.

Writers discussing the Old Testament a few decades ago used to observe that it was difficult for a modern reader to develop a "feel" for royal motifs in the Old Testament. They declared that we did not understand kingship as did citizens of 19th-century Britain or of Czarist Russia. True enough. But those persons did not understand kingship as it existed in Old Testament times. For the kingship of the Old Testament was influenced by the Canaanite world and the world of the Babylonian-Assyrian Empire.

It is easy enough for the modern reader to see how Old Testament kingship would be influenced by royal motifs operative throughout Canaan where Old Testament royalty came to flourish. It is more difficult to see how Babylonian themes could have been operative. To see this, one must understand something about cultural "channels of transmission" in the ancient Near East. Despite the absence of modern communications and transportation, these cultural and intellectual channels did exist. Ideas moved across boundaries with the same ease—if not with the same speed—as in our day. At least two significant groups of persons were "internationalist" in outlook: members of the scribal schools, and members of the guilds which formed religious personnel. Since both of these groups would have worked intimately with kings, ideas of kingship moved easily throughout the Mediterranean world.

Royal scribes, seated in chambers near the king, carried on correspondence with their like in other lands. Royal priest-chaplains, working in the temple—which was always to some extent a royal chapel—brought with them the religious cultural patterns which they or their fathers had acquired roaming from land to land in search of employment. Some of the royal themes were blurred in transmission. But these channels made possible the vestiges or "footprints" of such themes as the sacral king, the humiliated, dying, and resurrected king that we find in the Old Testament.

Remythologisation

Quite properly some years back, an eminent German scripture scholar won fame for himself by calling for demythologisation of the New Testament. Understanding *myth* from one perspective, he saw it as the accretion of materials around an historical core, and he saw the value of searching for that core. He saw that the accretions had taken on a life of their own and that from a certain perspective this was distressing, at least to a scholarly analysis of the New Testament.

But there is another aspect to myth. Myth can be the expression of those deep truths that are too painful or too complicated to be otherwise explained. If that is so, one demythologises at one's peril. The botanist sees value in the careful dissection of an orchid. Yet as a human being contemplating the disassembled parts, he realizes that something has been lost in the process. (And that something is life!) If myth is the expression of an ineffable truth, then by definition to demythologise is to attempt to discover the expressible part of the inexpressible. It results in scant profit. To demythologise is to desacralise. To desacralise is to destroy a large area of reality.

Demythologisation is not totally new. The Old Testament began the process of demythologising sex by moving away from fertility cults. (The New Testament remythologised sex by abstention: It propounded the Virgin Birth and the Celibacy of Christ the Rabbi in a world where marriage was demanded of the rabbi.) By ever-increasing insistence on the sacredness of marriage, the Old Testament compensated for its demythologisation of sex. It was left to the secularism of the current age to complete a process begun—innocently enough—in reaction against fertility cults.

But as this page is written, there is encouraging evidence that sex is being remythologized in the modern world. Still, the above discussion is reflective, and much of scripture is not. The world of the New Testament had, in our judgment, deep archetypal memories of the sacral king. He was—and all these words mean different things to different people—the son of God, the divine son, the adoptive son. He played a lead in the cult which brought "redemption." Although he so helped to bring redemption, he was himself "judge" as well as "king."

And it was against the backdrop of all these ideas that the early church preached and the New Testament taught.

12

God's Servant

Against the backdrop of material presented in the preceding chapter, this one will begin by citing a bit of the New Testament material. The early Christians, reflecting on their experience of Christ in faith, were reminded of another great theme from the Old Testament: God's servant. "For the Son of Man has come not to accept service but to give it and to give his life also as a ransom for many" (*Mk.* 10:45). The use of the term "many" (*polloi* in Greek) is a direct translation for the Hebrew word *"rabbim,"* used five times in one of the four "Servant Songs" in the Old Testament. The "many" is a Semitic idiom meaning "all." At least in Isaiah 53:10, there is a nearly direct expression (clearer in the ancient Greek text, perhaps, than in the Hebrew) that the servant will be a "ransom" for the sins of many.

In any event, there were at least four "songs" in the book of Isaiah that reminded the early church of Christ. These songs are: Isaiah 42:1-4, 49:1-6, 50:4-9, and 52:13—53:12. The songs are nothing if not mysterious. They speak of someone or several persons who had a special relationship to the Divinity: He was formed in the womb by the Divinity, called from the womb to a special and mysterious life. And that life was to suffer. The central personage(s) of these songs is basically innocent, but the Divinity wishes suffering for him despite all signs of innocence. Certainly there is here some alluding to the perennial problem of the "suffering of the just man," but there is far more than that.

With the New Testament use of these songs, we meet squarely with the problem of *exegesis* vs. *hermeneutics*. The former, as these terms are commonly used today, deals with the prob-

lems in getting the meaning that a text had for the original author or authors. In light of our earlier treatment of oral and
Semitic composition, it is obvious that it is not easy to phrase
even the *status quaestionis* with exegesis. At what time-frame
in the composition are we talking about when we speak of the
"meaning" of the author? Obviously if a given author took over
existing songs, he would use them for his own purpose. A further rewriting might modify the "meaning" with which exegesis would preoccupy itself.

Hermeneutics deals with still another question, "what is the
meaning of the text for the here and now?" After we have
deciphered the author's original meaning as well as we can,
and without being untrue to the original, what special meaning
does the text have for us at the present moment? Hermeneu-
tical questions are not limited to theological texts or treat-
ments of religious issues. When a legal document is written by
a group of men (let us think of the Constitution of the United
States), the document is a product of much discussion and
compromise. Presumably there were almost as many views as
to what the finished document meant as there were participants in the writing of the text. But the finished text has a life of
its own. The meaning of the text, should quarrels later arise, is
not determined by repolling the original legislators (even in
cases where that might be possible). Rather, it is determined
by serious study of the document that exists.

In this chapter we are studying the reasonable meaning of
the songs of Isaiah on a variety of levels. What did they mean
for the original writers, i.e., those who incorporated the songs
into a special context in the book of Isaiah? What did they
mean throughout the history of Jewish interpretation? What
use did the New Testament make of these songs? How legiti-
mate was that use? What are the meanings of songs for us
today as they exist in the Old Testament, studied without
benefit of New Testament interpretation?

Such questions can be asked in the dimension of a special
"faith-stance" or apart from it. For example, Christians who
see the Lord of History moving graciously but powerfully in the
affairs of men would have no difficulty in seeing him using an-

cient authors to point to the One who was to come. A faith-stance of another person might see special religious meaning in the Old Testament, but might be amused (or annoyed) by New Testament use of the material. A person with no faith-stance at all can still puzzle over the meanings that these texts had for the religious groups which assembled and transmitted them.

Sometimes Christians have difficulty understanding Jewish annoyance with the Christian use of the Old Testament. And yet how would Christians feel if an alien religious denomination were to gain domination in the areas of the world we live in by using the New Testament in the following manner? "Christians are basically fine people, but they do not understand the meaning of the New Testament. Our new religious group—while continuing to think kindly thoughts of the Christians as persons will begin now to use the New Testament as it ought properly to be used." That patronizing attitude toward the Old Testament and Jewish use of the Old Testament has been common throughout Christian history. Moreover, it has been coupled to a total lack in awareness of Jewish theological growth since Old Testament times. Unfortunately, the dimensions of the resulting problems for a genuine ecumenical relationship between Jew and Christian lie far beyond the scope of this book. Perhaps by simple advertence to the existence of the problem, we are accomplishing something.

The Servant and Vicarious Punishment

The notion of vicarious punishment can be stated bluntly: "By his stripes we are healed . . . the Lord placed on him the guilt which belongs to us all" (*Is.* 53:5-6). This theme is seen throughout the latter three of the songs. Prescinding now for a moment from the Christian notion of the redemptive suffering and death of Christ, can this line make any sense in a religious context? What is "guilt?" What is it to be "healed?" How is it possible for one person to be "healed" through the chastisement of someone who is innocent?

The Old Testament is not an ideal pedagogue. For one thing, it works on the presumption that a number of things are absolutely obvious. If the reader of the Old Testament has to have these things explained, the Old Testament assumes that he probably would not be able to understand them anyway, and so the Old Testament never bothers to explain. A number of these presumptions must be spelled out if the above song is to make any sense at all.

First of all, the Old Testament presumes the absolute unity of the human family. It seems at times to speak of the human family as an individual. This is part of the problem in our grappling with the mystery of "original sin" in the Old Testament. While we are asking ourselves, "How is it possible for all mankind to suffer through the fault of an individual?", the Old Testament answers—if it hears our question at all—"How could anything else be possible?" This is the other side of the coin. If there is "guilt"—and there is—how can mankind possibly approach the Divinity without first accepting punishment? What is the nature of that guilt and that punishment? In the "Servant Song" context, the Old Testament is not so much concerned with the guilt of personal sins—with direct violations of God's law and consequent harm to our neighbor—as with the general Old Testament proclamation that humanity stands somehow under judgment.

With this idea of "standing under judgment," we touch an experience that is known to most of us from reading testimonies from holy persons of almost any religious denomination. Viewed from our standpoint, they are extraordinarily good persons. Their protestations in their diaries, let us say, of their "sinfulness," their descriptions of themselves as "the worst of sinners," strike the ear harshly. Most of us are inclined to look to Freud or other psychologists for explanations of this preoccupation with "guilt" where—in our judgment—there manifestly is none.

Perhaps there is another explanation. In a book written around the turn of the century, Professor Rudolph Otto spoke of the *Idea of the Holy* as it occurs in various world religions. He saw as the least common denominator of the Divinity that

he was *quid tremendum*—"something to be trembled at." Otto
saw, running through a variety of major religions, the notion
that God was Other, and that the nature of his holiness was to
be "totally different." Possibly this explains the difference in
our judgment of ourselves and the judgment that extremely
holy persons make of themselves. Most of us, when we engage
in sporadic self-examination, compare ourselves to others and
find ourselves not appreciably worse. The especially saintly
person does not spend much time in such comparisons. He
compares himself with the Living God. Moreover, because he
stands so much closer to the Divinity than the rest of us do, he
knows the Divinity much better and sees the Divinity—if not as
he is—far more clearly than the rest of us do. And he trembles.

The Old Testament is sympathetic with this approach. It
gives little comfort to a person who compares himself with his
fellows and finds the results not too distressing. It urges him to
compare himself with the Divinity. If the reader of the Old
Testament does not tremble then, the Old Testament is not
much interested in him any longer.

But if he does tremble? Then there is hope, for he realizes
that he is indeed "under judgment": he realizes that he bears
heavy guilt and that he lacks any means of taking that guilt
away. The reader of the Old Testament is not depressed by
these notions. First of all, because the views of "guilt and punishment" reinforce the Old Testament's views of the twofold
dimension of "filial" fear. (I must obey the Divinity, the Father, or all sorts of unspecified bad things may happen to me.
On the other hand, *if I fear him, I need fear no one else.* My
Father has the same power over all men that he has over me.)

Secondly, the awareness of guilt and the deservedness of
punishment is not morbid because of the next dynamic that it
led to. Later Jewish writing interprets it in the following manner: At the Last Judgment one of the first questions that will
be asked is, "Did you hope intensely for Salvation?" Hope is
expected. To be aware that one is guilty is not such a fearful
thing, if one has a founded hope of being forgiven.

In the context of the Servant Songs, how will this forgiveness
come about? The longest of the songs (*Is.* 52:13—53:12) spells

it out in some detail. It must be admitted at the beginning that the Hebrew of these passages is more than ordinarily troublesome. This could hardly be otherwise. The interpretation of these songs changed even from their earliest versions. Consequently, there was always the temptation for a redactor to make the slightest vowel change (an easy matter in Hebrew, where the vowels were orally transmitted long after the consonants were written) in order to make the entire song more consonant with the total theme which the redactor had accepted as the clue to the meaning. Still, the following reasonably honest effort at translation may serve:

Who could have believed what we have heard? (*Is.* 53:1)
. . .
No form had he or stateliness (*Is.* 53:2)
Despised and forsaken of men
A man of sorrows and familiar with pain
And as one from whom men avert their gaze.
He was despised and we regarded him not. (*Is.* 53:3)
Yet ours was the sickness he bore
and ours the pain he suffered. (*Is.* 53:4)
He was pierced through by reason of our rebellions
Crushed by reason of our iniquities.
The chastisement of our betterment was on him.
By his stripes there is healing for us. (*Is.* 53:5)
All of us like sheep had gone astray
. . . And JHWH caused to light on him
the iniquity of us all. (*Is.* 53:6)
After arrest and sentence he was taken off. (*Is.* 53:8)
And his death was among the wicked (*Is.* 53:9)
Yes, JHWH was pleased to crush him.
Truly he gave himself as a guilt-offering. (*Is.* 53:10)
After his travail of soul, he shall see light.
He shall redeem through his sweat.
My servant shall bring justification to many.
And their iniquities he shall bear. (*Is.* 53:11)

It may be mentioned briefly in passing that certain specifics

must have at least excited the early church: the physical de-
formity, the idea of "death among the wicked." Yet these
parallels must not be over-stressed. What truly impressed the
early church was the conviction that the Christ whom she had
experienced had brought justification to many persons by bear-
ing their iniquities and by suffering for them. Two extremes are
to be avoided here. We would avoid the "detective story"
aspect of the Old Testament. On the other hand, we would not
lose sight of the fact that the Old Testament (crystallized now
in this one song) is aware of human guilt and punishment
merited and points to the possibility of "vicarious suffering."
Reflecting on this, the early church saw an affinity between the
themes of this and the other songs and the experience that she
had of the Christ that suffered and died for the sins of men and
who, after his travail of soul, saw light.

One theological parallel here—far deeper than mere external
details—is that the "meritorious pain" of the servant is woven
together with his own personal vindication. Hebrew tenses are
fluid, but the moment of the intercessory expiation seems to be
identical with the servant's personal triumph. This is interesting to Christians in light of contemporary insistence that the
death and resurrection of Christ are not to be viewed as discrete and unrelated acts but as constituents of the one redemption. Led on by the Servant Songs, the early church may have
realized that doctrine more clearly than some passages of scripture seem to indicate. (There are other texts, of course, in the
New Testament which make the union of death and resurrection quite clear, e.g., Romans 4:25.) Jewish reaction against the
Christian use of these passages was quite strong for many centuries. For reasons that we have explained already, the reaction
is perfectly understandable.

Still, the Christian interpretation of Christ as the suffering
servant flows from an understandable religious dynamic. If the
Divinity is the *quid tremendum* and man is aware of his own
sinfulness, there are only a few general ways of handling the
resulting tension. One, of course, is simply to conclude that
man is so weak, so incapable of "proper actions," that he will
not be punished for transgressions. An analogous mode is to

conclude that, while man perhaps bears some measure of responsibility, a general amnesty of some sort is ever available to mankind. The third modality is to assume that man is capable of good actions, but that he frequently fails. The punishment which he deserves for his sins falls in some fashion on another person. Many readers see this last modality operating in the Servant Songs.

But although that modality in treating the Servant Songs has been rejected by large areas of Jewish thought through the centuries, an appreciation of vicarious punishment has emerged in another fashion. Ancient Jewish legend, flowing at least from Talmudic times, comes to speak of the *Lamedvavnikim*, the thirty-six just men. (*Lamed-vav* in Hebrew means simply thirty-six.) These men live in every age. And they are righteous. It is for their sake that the Divinity does not destroy the world. They are innocent, and they suffer. One of the ways in which they suffer is that they do not know that they are among the thirty-six just men. When suffering comes their way, it may be accompanied by the fear that they deserve to suffer for some "hidden sin."

We have spoken here of "legend," and the term should not offend the reader. There are non-Jewish facets in the origin of the *Lamedvavnikim*. (The thirty-six is probably derived from Babylonian mathematics and calendar-writing.) But the message of the legend is basically the same as that of the Servant Songs. Why do just men suffer? And the answer supplied is, among other reasons, because sin must be punished. The difficulty with punishing sinners is that they are ignorant and obstinate. Even if the Divinity were to punish them, they would not improve, and his desire is to heal all men. So he punishes the just. They profit from it, and the human family stands the chance of becoming well.

One may be puzzled by this. But if one grants that the human family is one, that the Divinity is awesomely holy, and that man is weak, sinful, and in need of correction, the solution does hold together in a strange but beautiful fashion.

Jewish writing has been reluctant to see the suffering servant precisely as a Messiah. (Jewish writing, correctly, sees the Old Testament dealing with a plurality of Messiahs, but is reluctant to identify a single Messiah as suffering redemptively.) It has striven rather to see the servant as the embodiment of the Hebrew people, as a group of individuals, or as a special individual in time subsequent to the writing of the Songs. (Reminding ourselves, for a moment, of the *exegesis* and *hermeneutics* dichotomy, it can almost be said that to identify a precise historical individual in connection with one of these songs—could such an identification be made—is almost without interest in light of subsequent usage of the songs. If the songs did originate in reflecting on the sufferings of one obscure Hebrew, theological reflection makes the original "servant" almost insignificant.)

The Servant as Israel

As was noted in the discussion of the *Lamedvavnikim*, the pious find suffering ever so much more tolerable if assured that they are not being punished for their own sins. Surely this is the dynamic that has made a deep feeling for the *Lamedvavnikim* so popular among Jews. Moreover, the experience of our generation with the holocaust—the death of six million Jews at the hands of the Nazis—has the current age understandably obsessed with a desperate effort to find meaning in horror. The pain of reflection is so great in this regard that we move on quickly. Can the Lord of History move in the midst even of such horror and inhumanity to attain his ends? Many who have written either on the servant or on the *Lamedvavnikim* insist that he can. There are persons who shrink from such a statement, being so appalled that they cannot bring themselves away from the six million to reflect for a moment on the power of the God that Lives, the power that can bring goodness even out of horror. For them one can only have the deepest sympathy and acceptance.

If it is not blasphemous to move from the six million to contemporary life . . . all good men may be called to some share in suffering for the good of mankind. Fully conscious of his oft-expressed belief that the death and resurrection of Christ were fully redemptive, Paul of Tarsus still speaks of "making up the suffering yet lacking to Christ" (*Col.* 1:24). Threatened with death, scourged, imprisoned, Paul identified his own suffering somehow with that of the Christian servant figure.

In a recent work, Dr. Karl Menninger, famed American psychiatrist, asks the question (startling, coming from a psychiatrist), *Whatever Became of Sin*? He suggests that men grew weary of religion's preoccupation with a kind of holiness centering on the personal, the private, the lone individual. In the process, people lost sight of the real social dimension which sin has. So it is with religious polarities. It is true enough to say that the Old Testament continues to embrace contradictions, but men—at least at a given moment—cannot. They must opt for one or the other: the transcendent and awesome God or the one who dwells within, God's awesome holiness vis-á-vis man's sinfulness or his capacity to forgive man.

The profound beauty of the Servant Songs encompasses many things. It does not compromise the holiness of God but shows us that there is access to him, even for the sinful, through the ministry of those who are less sinful. It reinforces (although it does not explain) the mysterious unity of the human family. And it gives meaning to suffering. A poignant line from a successful novel of some years back, *The Man on a Donkey*, speaks of someone weeping like "a child that is beaten and does not know the reason why. . . ." The line evokes the deep human feeling that there is a special agony to that suffering which seems to have no explanation. Surely the Servant Songs as they have been understood in Jewish and Christian tradition do not solve the problem of suffering. (Who can calmly reflect within sight or sound of a suffering infant?) But they are an effort. Religious writings survive more easily if they afford some measure of comfort. Here, as often in the Old Testament, the comfort offered is calculated largely to soothe only the strong, but it is a real comfort nonetheless.

The Servant in the New Testament

The early Christians insisted that Christ was the fulfillment of Old Testament promise. In their reconstruction of his conversations they note that he permitted or accepted things that happened because "it is written of him" (*Mk.* 14:21) or "that the Scriptures might be fulfilled" (*Mk.* 14:49). In light of our discussion of the Suffering Servant, the passage from Emmaus road takes on clear meaning. "But he said to them: 'O foolish and slow of heart to believe in all that the prophets have spoken! Did not Christ have to suffer these things and so enter into his glory?' And beginning with Moses (the Pentateuch) and all the prophets, he interpreted to them in all the Scriptures the things referring to himself" (*Lk.* 24:25-27). We have already cited the passage of the one who came to give service, not to receive it—and to give his life also as a ransom for many (*Mk.* 10:45). Luke 22:26 points this "service" out in concrete detail. "Who is of higher rank? The one who sits at table or the one who serves . . .? I am with you as one that serves."

Many other texts throughout the gospels and epistles could be cited as proof that the early church saw an identity between Christ and the servant of the Isaian songs. We shall not cite them. It is no disservice to Jesus of Nazareth, himself a pious Jew, or to the Christ of faith, to suggest sober reflection on the Servant Songs without advertence to the New Testament. To live a human existence—with or without a faith-stance—is to be exposed to suffering. The Isaian songs present the reflections of a wise, wise people, exposed to much suffering. The songs that they wrote for Isaiah grew out of that suffering. The songs were an effort to make the suffering significant. Much that we said in the earlier parts of the book about oral and social composition are enough to justify speculation that these songs are the result of the same process. Moreover, there is so much wisdom in them that one is reluctant to think of them as the contributions of an individual:

> For masterpieces are not single and solitary births; they are the outcome of many years of thinking in common, of thinking by the body of the people, so that the experience of the mass is behind the single voice.
>
> Virginia Woolf, *A Room of One's Own*

13

The Prophet

In reflecting on her experience of Christ, the early Church was often reminded of one experience that perdured throughout the history of Israel—the contact of the community with God through the prophets. The prophetic role took sundry shapes. This is hardly surprising in light of the length of the history of Israel (until Christian times and after), the variety of religious experiences which were hers, and the demands which the people of Israel made at one moment or another on their religious leadership.

The fruits of these reflections for the Christian Church were many. In reflecting on Christ, Christians had a wide variety of happy religious memories to dip into, a treasure-house of *nova et vetera* with which to describe the experience of the Christ-encounter that had been theirs. Consequently, the Church could easily describe Christ in terms of the experience that the assembly of Israel had had with the prophets. By the same token, however, since that experience of Israel with the prophets was so diverse, and since the Church was so selective in her use of those experiences, we cannot argue with any degree of precise logic that Christ was the prophet of whom the Old Testament spoke. Nor can we contend that those who fail to see such logic suffer from "hardened hearts."

It is a fact, of course, that any given portrayal of the prophet in the Old Testament texts was written with a specific audience in mind. Consequently, it is only with a great deal of caution that one can uncover themes that seem to be common to a large variety of texts and to distill from these themes something that is common to prophecy *in genere*. Still, there is a certain validity to this procedure, as long as the common denominator one chooses is broad enough to be truthfully applied to all areas of prophecy. Two such areas are fairly easy to find. We might call them prophecy as warning and prophecy as comfort.

Prophecy as Warning

A common theme of all the great prophets is that Jahweh is coming to judge his people. While surely the great message of Jahweh's relentless love must cover even these threats, some of them bear a terrible finality about them, such as the use of the term "the end" in Amos and Ezekiel.

> The end has come on my people Israel;
> I will never again come by them (*Amos* 8:2).

The end has come on the four corners of the land. Now the end is on you. I shall unleash my anger on you and will punish you for your ways and for all your abominations" (*Ezek.* 7:2-3).

For Hosea, Israel is no longer Jahweh's folk (*Hos.* 1:9). Similar texts may be piled up as examples. Jeremiah sees even a certain "hatred" developing in Jahweh for his people (*Jer.* 12:7-8). Again, for Hosea "compassion is hid" from the eyes of Jahweh who must stop and ask himself if he ought to ransom his people from the power of death, from the grasp of Sheol, from the plagues, from the destruction (*Hos.* 13:14). Jahweh comes to punish his people who are warned: Prepare to meet your doom! (*Amos* 4:12). Yet these texts, as we noted in *The Threshing Floor*, should not be exaggerated. If it is true that Jahweh comes to punish—as his prophet insists—it is nonetheless true that *he comes*. By speaking of the approaching punishment, the prophet speaks also of the approaching Divinity. "Did ever a people have a god so near to them as the Lord is to you?" (*Deut.* 4:7). True enough, the question in Deuteronomy is framed in another context. But even the prophecies of warning cannot be isolated from the notion that they speak of a God that comes—even if he comes to chastise. It is not totally apart from this context that Matthew's gospel has the Baptist putting the question: "Who has shown you to flee the approaching wrath?" The wrath that approaches may well be the coming Christ (or the eschatological Christ)—the prophet and the message now one—as the early Church reread the Old Testament. We must be careful, though, not to miss the implied comfort even in the wrathful question. The early Church—temporarily vexed with the synagogue down the street—sometimes missed the comfort implied in the question that the Baptist echoed from the earlier prophets.

The Comfort

The prophets who uttered these dire warnings are joined by others uttering messages of warmth, and hope, and solace. In some cases, the same prophets who had spoken of wrath and misery to their disciples (who lovingly gathered the sayings and preserved them in their "schools"), spoke also of subsequent consolation. Perhaps a simple explanation of this dichotomy is available. The prophets played the roles of affective authority figures in any society (such as parents, teachers, clergymen). Before the awful event, they threaten of the wrath that is to come in the hope that it may be forestalled. Once it has come, however, it has come. No amount of tongue-lashing will undo the damage. So now these same figures speak in terms of warmth and consolation that the event, whatever it might be, may not be destructive but medicinal in its punitive effect.

Second Isaiah is bold enough (*Is.* 43:18f, 48:6, 54:4) to urge his hearers not even to think of the Lord's great deeds of the past but to look to a new deed which will make the past ones look weak and vapid. The earlier prophecy that "A remnant will return" (*Is.* 7:3) offered stern comfort. It promised less than total destruction. There would be a remnant to return. But only a remnant. Other great themes of hope that echo through the prophets are that Israel will be "resurrected" (e.g., *Ezek.* 37:7-14), or that Israel will be "chosen again" (*Is.*

14:1). These great themes are allusive and poetically vague. Surely the faithful have seen them fulfilled many times in Jewish history (including the existence of the modern state of Israel). If they have not judged them to be perfectly fulfilled, they have looked with love and with trust to a farther future when the God who is faithful and true will indeed fill up all his promises.

The pious Jew who was the "average member" of the Christian assembly in her earliest days could only look to both of these groups of themes—the prophet who warns, the prophet who consoles—and see that the Christ of his faith was easily described in these majestic Old Testament terms.

Sitting in God's Council

One of the finest contemporary writers on Old Testament themes has made the observation that prophets were esteemed in Israel or were not esteemed regardless of whether their prophecies came true or did not come true. Rather, he notes, they were revered because when they spoke "they spoke with the voice of Jahweh." This is a brilliant insight. The purpose of the prophet is not to guarantee that the people who listen to him will prosper, but that they will do God's will. It may or may not be God's will here and now that his people will prosper. More complicated yet, the true prophet may urge on his hearers a course of action. They accept the course of action. Subsequent events make clear that another course of action would have been wiser and would have resulted—from certain perspectives—in a happier issue. No matter. If the prophet spoke with the voice of Jahweh, it was simply the Lord's will that that particular course of action be followed. That was the divine wisdom for a particular moment in history. If it led to poor results, as seen from one perspective, even those poor results may have been intended by the Divinity who viewed all this from a totally different perspective.

It is not always given to the prophet to see what God's perspective is. He is often called to preach a particular mode of action without a vision of where the action leads or what the value of it is. Still, the true prophet shares some vision of what the Lord is about, for he has sat with the Lord in his *sod*, his council. The image is an ancient Semitic one: The great chief sits with his advisers. Even if he devises a plan that is all his own, they are instructed in its reasoning. The image is clearer in the Ugaritic material where the Lord himself sits surrounded by "divine beings," but there are vestiges of this in the Old Testament (*Gen.* 1:26, 1 *Kings* 22:19ff, *Job* 1:6ff). The active role of the "counsellor" here must not be overstated. No man can instruct God, for, as Isaiah asks: "Who has directed the Spirit of the Lord, or as his counsellor has really taught him?" (*Is.* 40:13). Still, Jeremiah says of false prophets—speaking in the name of the Lord—"If they had stood in my *sod*, they would have preached my words to my people" (*Jer.* 23:22). In other words, the mysterious sharing of the vision of what it is that the Lord wants done, the insight, however obscure, of the direction in which the Lord is leading makes the true prophet true. Again, Jeremiah charges the false prophets: "Which of them has stood in the council of the Lord so that they could perceive his word?" (*Jer.* 23:18). And Amos sees the *sod* as the results of these deliberations: "Surely the Lord Jahweh does nothing without revealing his *sod* (i.e., the end-product of the *sod*) to his servants the prophets" (*Amos* 3:7). As the notion of the transcendence of Jahweh grew more and more in Hebrew thought, so did the active notion of the *sod* grow less and less. From the "divine beings" of the earlier passages, from the active counsellors in the Ugaritic material who give the chief deity hard advice, the prophets became "overhearers" of the word, who, having sat, passively but really, at the *sod* where Jahweh proclaimed his intentions, were capable of explaining his will to his people. Both the Hebrew word for prophet, *nabi'*, and the Greek word *prophetes* used by the Septuagint to translate the Hebrew, carry solid evidence for the meaning of prophets as "forth-tellers," "speakers-out" of God's word, rather than fore-tellers or fortune-tellers. The function of the true prophet who had sat in the *sod* of the Lord was to tell his people what ought to be done now. Whether that doing would have a happy issue, as men judge happy issues, was really not very important. Frequently throughout the New Testament, Jesus is seen as participating with the Father in his *sod*, "before the world was" (cf. *Jn.* 17:5). Having so participated, he was enabled to speak forth with the voice of Jahweh.

Moses the Forthteller

When Moses brings two tablets of the law down from his encounter with the Divinity, another aspect of the prophet is revealed (e.g., *Ex.* 31:18). There are two tables of the law; *probably each of them is complete in itself.* This is a throwback to the tradition of other covenantal relations in the ancient Near East where two identical copies of the stipulations of the covenant would be written. One of them would be kept by the greater power, the other by the lesser, so that each might be aware of what the commitments were. Later Old Testament traditions got confused on this, and both tables were kept in a liturgical shrine, but it is a well-founded intuition which suggests that, in its earliest form, the prophet kept one tablet and the people the other. The prophet Moses, who had truly sat in God's *sod* and consequently understood the function of the commandments as a non-prophet could not, kept the copy as the vicegerent of the Great Lord Jahweh who dwelt at a distance and who could not therefore be expected, as would an ordinary king, to keep his own copy of the covenant.

Against this backdrop then, the picture of Christ as the new Moses—which he is for Matthew certainly—takes on further color. It is not simply that Christ is being presented as the new lawgiver (and Matthew's gospel as a latter-day pentateuch), but Christ is one who has sat in the *sod* of the Divinity; he himself bears his own copy of the Lord's covenant within his person. By comparing one's own actions with those of the Christ of Faith, one can judge whether or not one is himself faithful and true to the stipulations.

Samuel: Child-Prophet, Liturgical Reformer

The first three chapters of the first book of Samuel are complex and rich. They contain some heavy-handed rewriting of earlier traditions. The chapters are certainly partially motivated by a desire to show Samuel, even as a child, showing flashes of the prophetic greatness of his mature years. The chapters are charming. There is something extraordinary about his birth. What is impossible with man is not impossible with God, and so Samuel comes into the world. At a very early age he finds himself in the Temple of the Lord. The Divinity speaks to him. He finds himself inevitably a reproach to those who have been, prior to him, appointed to the divine service. His fidelity to his appointed tasks is obviously contrasted to the avarice of those who had been appointed to liturgical service before him.

As we noted, the chapters of Samuel have been much rewritten, and their original intent is not totally clear. (Nor certainly was its written form much clearer in New Testament times.) Consequently, with confidence we can point to a few allusions in the New Testament and suggest the possibility that these were designed to trigger emotional explosions deep within the Jewish-Christian psyche. The finding of the Child Jesus in the Temple (*Lk*. 2:46ff), his later wrathful scourging of the unclean from the Temple precincts (*Mt*. 21:12), his life-long conflict with at least some of the Pharisees and some of the priests— surely the New Testament intended that this should remind its hearers of something. The something is this: No religious movement that grows from another does so easily. It must establish its legitimacy. This can be done only in a few ways. The new movement can assert that the Divinity has thrust himself into history and upset his own ordered plan, or it can show that this "new religion" is a perfectly logical sequel of all that the Divinity has done hitherto. It is humanly easier to maintain these arguments if one insists that the previously privileged members of a religious class have not been faithful to their position and that it has consequently been taken away from them. Unfortunately, in dealings of Christians with Jews, this belief has occasionally run away with itself—more often on the popular level than on the theological. Still, there are theological threads in the New Testament that can easily lead to anti-Semitism. John's gospel, for example, with all its theological precision, regularly speaks of "the Jews" when it really means, "this handful of Jews" or even "this symbol of all those who are not interested in the Christ of Faith." Most religious persons (in which group we may include "devout atheists") harbor the feeling that we are not as faithful to our religion as we ought to be. This feeling is, unfortunately but humanly, assuaged by persuading ourselves that others are even worse than we. (Thus the reference to the devout atheists who spend much time condemning the non-Sunday behavior of faithful churchgoers.) As a result of this nearly universal human weakness we have a strange dynamic that flows from the religion of the New Testament. It begins by taking the best of the Old Testament, such as Moses and Samuel, and comparing them unfavorably with the Christ of Faith. The resulting attitude lent strength to the dynamic that came to think bitterly of Jews and to treat them harshly. Ironic. Unfortunately, there seems to be some foundation to the cynical dictum that "God is a grand person. It is his friends that I cannot stand."

Proclamation as Confrontation

The common Hebrew memory of the prophet pictured him as someone with unusual authority. It was not only that he proclaimed the word of God or that he spoke with the voice of Jahweh, but that he forced decision. Life could not simply flow on as it did once the prophet stepped into its current. The word of God could be heard or rejected, but a decision had to be made. "How long will you hesitate between two sides, if the Lord be God then follow him, but if Baal, then follow him" (1 *Kings* 18:21). One is no longer offered the chance to wait just a bit longer and to see how it turns out so that one may "go with the winner." While the New Testament shows Christ in almost constant confrontation, the tale of the "rich young man" (*Lk.* 18:18ff) is an especially classic example of prophetic challenge. The man was well-disposed, leading a life of considerable asceticism and wishing to stand closer to the Master. He is told the price and goes sadly away. There is no calling after him. There is no reduction in price announced. There is no reassurance that the glories are worth the price. The word is proclaimed. It is heard or ignored, and the prophet moves on. "He whom God has sent speaks God's words for to him has God given the Spirit without measure or restraint" (*Jn.* 3:34). And he speaks it, and one hears or one does not. And he teaches them as one who has authority (*Mt.* 7:29). Some twenty references in the gospel texts proclaim that Christ had authority, that (some) people recognized his authority, that he delegated some of that authority to his apostles, that his authority extended to the ability to teach, to correct, to rule demons, to govern natural events. This authority is not without prior parallel, but it has —in the preaching of the early church—never been possessed in such degree (cf. *Heb.* 1:1).

Wonder-Working

It is largely in connection with prophetic authority that the role of the thaumaturge, the wonder-worker, comes into play. It is not enough to claim authority. "What is easier to say, 'Your sins are forgiven you' or 'Get up and walk.' 'But that you may know that the Son of Man has power over sin on earth . . . Get up and walk,' he said to the crippled man" (*Lk.* 5:24). So rarely are the powers of the wonder-worker used for himself, that some writers say that this is one of the characteristics of the wonder-working power as a sign and stamp of authority. It is interesting to note that Franz Werfel, of pious Jewish stock, cited this tendency in his fictionalized biography *Song of Bernadette.* Dying painfully, Bernadette listened with some patience to the suggestions that she allow herself to be brought to the healing waters of Lourdes. There, it is recalled, if she did not insist that she spoke with the voice of Jahweh, at least she insisted that she had his message mediately. For Bernadette, the healing powers of the waters were secondary; they were a sign that her "messages" calling for prayer, penance, reform were authoritative. But she insisted also that "the waters are not for me," that she was not to be so healed. In the prophetic tradition, she realized that it is not the role of the teaching physician to heal himself. The prophet is to be an "assayer and tester" of other folk (*Jer.* 6:27) and clearly an intercessor (*Gen.* 20), but it is part of the tradition that while he may save others, himself he cannot save.

Against this background, then, the New Testament speaks of Christ as prophet. It proclaims him as having this vision of himself. He will not alter his itinerary out of fear of Herod, "for it cannot be that a prophet perish outside of Jerusalem" (i.e., he will soon perish) (*Lk.* 13:33). Luke also narrates the resurrection of the son of the widow of Naim (*Lk.* 7:11-17) in an account that parallels Elias and the son of the widow of Sarepta. Mark quotes Jesus as saying of himself: "No prophet lacks honor, except in his own country, among his brethren, in his own house" (*Mk.* 6:4). At least a dozen times, the New Testament uses the term "prophet" or "the prophet" in some approving way in talking about Jesus of Nazareth.

Far more important than the use of the name is the description of Christ's activities. He speaks in the name of the Lord, announces his judgments, proclaims his will. He lives in another world as well as this one (cf. *Lk.* 10:18-21). He understands the mysteries of the human heart. He speaks to that heart "in the voice of Jahweh."

There is one further complication to the role of Christ the prophet in the New Testament. Some of this deals with a "coming age" and with the activity of Christ the eschatological prophet. The Son of Man who was to come on the clouds of heaven was expected in a very near future. When that future grew clearly to be a more distant one, the Church reflected further on her memories of his words. She did not understand them fully. She reflected more. She is reflecting still.

However she viewed Christ, it must be remembered that the Church—as do we—could recognize only something that she had seen before. If the Church had not been so Jewish, she would have experienced Christ in other terms. But she was Jewish, and so did she experience him, partially at least, as servant of God, sacral king, and prophet. Those were the types swirling around the formation of the common Hebrew psyche.

All of their dimensions were not always written on the formulated pages of the Old Testament, as we have remarked often, but they were otherwise recorded. It was in terms of this other recording, a deep-rooted psychological recollection, that the church remembered and was able to recognize the one who was to come.

> The rain and snow come down from Heaven. They do not return then to Heaven until they have first watered the earth and made it sprout, giving seed to them that sow and bread to them that eat. Even so with the word that goes forth from my mouth. It does not return to me "empty" without accomplishing that which I intended when I sent it forth (*Is.* 55:10-11).

It is difficult for the Christian to read this passage and not to suppose that the gospel of John the Divine, John the Theologian, made use of the image of God's word, that was with God, that came from God, and that returned to him, having left his people bread to eat. Indeed for John this word did not return to the Father without having accomplished the purpose for which it was sent forth. In other places where the New Testament speaks of the eucharist (1 *Cor.* 10:16-17, 1 *Cor.* 11:24, *Mt.* 26:26-29, *Mk.* 14:22-25, *Lk.* 22:14-20 and cf. *Ex.* 12:14, *Deut.* 16:3), there is veiled allusion to the role both of the "cultic prophet," the bread, and the living prophetic word.

In some ways, the quote from Isaiah above is a classic example of the relationship between Old Testament and New Testament which these chapters are trying to show. The two exist not precisely as cause and effect. The first suggests ideas to the second. The New Testament takes ideas from the Old Testament and weaves them into a pattern of its own, colored by these Old Testament ideas as they were on the written page and as they echoed in the chambers of the common Hebrew psyche which existed in New Testament times. In the judgment of the author of these chapters, this is a difficult concept and an elusive one. But it is valid.

Perhaps these last three chapters should not have been written. They were an effort to make "academically respectable" something which the Christian church did. They were an effort to legitimize—deliberately and reflectively—something which an entire community did with grace and ease and spontaneity, as though it were an act of nature. And how does one justify a sunrise? To some readers who are pious Christians, the chapters may seem arrogant. To readers who are pious members of other religions or who really do not care for the notion of religion at all, the chapters may seem to have been a waste of time.

But for the Christian who has some "feel" for the Jesuit religious tradition, the relentless quest to know at least the periphera that surround the unknowable, the thrust of the chapters will have been understandable. Cardinal Newman, himself a learned student of the scriptures, found the need of something outside the scriptures to make the whole intelligible. What that something might be and how it should be explained would rather belong to the area of what Roman Catholics now call "systematic theology" than to any of the themes with which this book directly concerns itself. Still for those that believe, Newman's seminal explanation may be mentioned: There is an author who writes and speaks and explains through human agents things that the humans did not always understand. So was it possible for Ugaritic themes to be incorporated into the Old Testament. So was it possible for the New Testament legitimately to adapt themes whose total meaning was not always clear to individual Old Testament authors. So is it possible, as religious life continues to grow, for contemporary individuals to find in the themes of the New Testament meanings somehow legitimately founded there that were not totally clear to the early church figures who preached and the audiences that actively listened.

14

A Children's Liturgy?

This chapter will be somewhat different from any of those read up until now. It will be an effort to rewrite, in discursive prose, something which was written by the author previously in more scientific jargon. Because this chapter is frankly more original than anything that has appeared in the book up to this point, it may, at some junctures, seem to contradict (or may contradict!) standard viewpoints previously presented. Perhaps it will be a good test for the reader's alertness to see how many of those contradictions he can find.

The standard view of *JEDP* has already been discussed. In an appendix to this volume, there has been printed a line-by-line listing of the verses which belong—in common judgment—to one source or another. It must be underlined that the appendix represents a standard opinion. There has been no tampering with the listings to make a thesis. These listings represent a fairly common opinion on which verses (for a variety of reasons) may be said to belong to one source or the other.

We are basically preoccupied here with the *"P"* source. Again, common opinion has tended to divide this source into two major divisions, the *P*-narrative and the *P*-legal material. We are chiefly concerned with the *P*-narrative. At this juncture, or at least after reading the chapter, the reader is well advised to take a chore on himself. He should sit down with any standard Old Testament version in English and mark the passages that are described as *P* in our appendix. When this is done, he should read the entire *P*-source from beginning to end. The reader will probably be surprised. First, he will find that the work can be read substantially as a whole in itself. His dark suspicions, if he has any, that *JEDP* is a creation of the scholarly mind with a thesis to prove, will probably evanesce.

The fact that one source can be read as a complete whole, with few yawning gaps, gives some credence to the *JEDP* theory. The division between *P*-narrative and *P*-legal may or may not be quite so clear to the reader. Probably it will be. Each of the two has a style all its own, and they are not easily confused. Moreover, the "reality content" of each is totally different. The passages in *P* which tell stories are really quite simple. The legal passages are different not only because they are legal, but because they are hopelessly complex. They are so complex (in descriptions of the Temple regulations, for example) that it is difficult to think of them as pertaining to any real world which ever existed. So the *P*-source breaks easily in two.

There is suasive argumentation that the *P*-narrative is far older than most scholars have deemed it hitherto. Students of comparative ancient literatures now insist that the oldest forms of writing are catalogues, mere lists of names. Later on, there is added to these lists some commentary, sometimes name by name. Then there occurs what these scholars call "literary coagulation." Only in a later stage are coherent stories formed around the smaller units (less or more skillfully), and a "united" whole then results. The seams sometimes show. In the *Odyssey*, for example, Odysseus is recognized some eight or nine times in the famed "recognition scene." One would have been fine; two or three would have been ample. But since each of these examples had grown slowly through the principle of coagulation, each had a powerful life of its own and would not die easily. The greatest single uniting literary feature of the *P*-narrative are the genealogies and name-lists—pointing back then to a fairly remote origin.

Now the question arises: For whom were the earliest forms of these sources written (*JEDP*, *P*-narrative and *P*-legal)? This chapter concerns itself basically with the *P*-narrative. The reader should not be kept in suspense. I believe that there is a version of the *P*-narrative, far earlier than the version which we have, that can still be detected in the current version. This earlier version was composed with one particular audience in mind, pubescent males in the Hebrew family. The narrative was composed as a kind of pious propaganda; it was designed to strengthen the young in their commitment to the Hebrew faith. Proximately, at one stage in its development, the narrative was intended to serve as the immediate preparation for adolescent circumcision. The Hebrew world—in common with most of the world of the ancient Near East—practiced adolescent, rather than the later infant circumcision.

This chapter is not polemical; in fact, some may feel that it is not particularly argumentative. Its argumentation is circuitous (not circular) but real. If originally the main thesis of the chapter rested on intuition, it should be noted that there is nothing illogical about intuition. Intuition is frequently strict logic with one or two steps in the logical process not yet explicitated.

A secondary confirmation of the thesis' validity is this: I began working with this material independently of any secondary sources. Only after much original work did I find parts of the thesis contained in the work of other scholars. [E.g., Sean McEvenue, (*The Narrative Style of the Priestly Writer*, Rome, 1971, PBI Press) and P. J. Budd, ("Priestly Instruction in Pre-Exilic Israel," *Vetus Testamentum* 23 [1973] 1-14).] Where I differ from these fine scholars will become clearer as the chapter unfolds.

What was the starting point of the work? In working with some Ugaritic material, I came on the following quotation which treats of one activity of *Dan'el*, a Ugaritic hero. "He is seated at the mouth of the opening among the noble ones who are on the threshing floor. He gives judgment to widows. He makes judgments for orphans." For a variety of reasons, threshing floors were sometimes used as judicial courts in the ancient Far Near East (cf. *1 Kings* 22:10). And there is extrabiblical evidence for this. Moreover, the threshing floor is also a site of cultic activity. It seemed not an impossible conjecture that the threshing floor was the center of some kind of *cultic judicial activity*. This was not sheer conjecture, due to the citing of the widows and orphans as precisely the persons involved in the judgment. Testimony throughout ancient Near Eastern documents bears eloquent witness to the (perhaps obvious) fact

that widows and orphans were much put upon in the ancient
world. They were defenseless, and in a society even more cruel
than is ours, they had few modes of recourse. In the Old Testament world, their recourse was the Lord. JHWH was the de-
fender of widow and orphan. To attack them was to attack
him. It seemed logical to suppose that this idea—like most Old
Testament ideas—was not original to the Old Testament but
came from somewhere else. In a *cultic* situation, even in a more
primitive society, there was some likelihood of enforcing an un-
popular judgment. One might be disposed to give to the widow
or the orphan that which was theirs not because one would not
prefer to keep their property for oneself, for example, but because the deity wished otherwise. This theory was at least con-
firmed by the meaning of the hero's name: *Dan'el*, "God
judges."

There may be a very clear confirmation of the above in
Psalm 82. The Hebrew of the short work is murky, but the following looks fairly probable as an explanation of the psalm's
meaning in its present mode. God stands in the divine assembly and he judges among the gods. He chides them for judging
unjustly. He specifically scolds them for judging unfairly the
fatherless and the needy. He tells the other gods that they will
die. The chorus cheers him on, "Arise God (the old battle-
cry), get up and judge the earth; you inherit the nations."

The above paraphrase is really a rather faithful echo of what
the Hebrew actually says. But one must overcome any embarrassment at the prospect of JHWH standing in an assembly of
gods and chiding them for not trying harder. What we probably
have here is an ancient pre-Hebraic song about a god or hero
(*Dan'el*?) standing in the divine assembly and chastising the
gods for not judging as they ought, and as he does. The lusty
cheer at the end was added by the pious Hebrew editor along
with an editorial comment (verse 5) on what happens when
lesser deities try to do their thing, "They know nothing; they
understand nothing; they stumble about in darkness and—
consequently—the foundations of the earth totter." (Gods are
powerful even when they make mistakes.) So Psalm 82 may
bear witness to the cult of which we speak.

There is a further step in the argumentation which will be

treated very briefly here: A judgment in favor of one party or the other could lead to a formulation of principles by which subsequent judgments could be made. Those principles then could be enforced by the same dynamic. They would be obeyed because they flowed from the cultic situation. They had been heard from the priest as from the representative of God, and they could not be ignored. One such set of principles might be the decalogue which we discussed in an earlier chapter.

While studying the Ugaritic material, I was reminded of a line from the *Bar Mitzvah* ritual where the father of the young man gives thanks that he is no longer responsible for the lad's responsibilities. The young boy is now responsible for himself. It must be cheerfully admitted that the Ugaritic threshing floor is a long way from the *Bar Mitzvah* ritual. (The Ugaritic material can be dated no later than the 13th century B.C.) But there is evidence that some themes of the *Bar Mitzvah* ritual are quite ancient. There are many references in Talmudic material to "obligation" beginning at thirteen. A precise reference to a man's being responsible for the sins of his son until the son is thirteen can be traced to Eleazar ben Simeon (2nd century A.D.). Moreover, it is a fairly sound principle of historiography to assume that a given dynamic continues beyond the point to which its tracing is "lost." In this case, how far can we trace the notion that the pubsecent Hebrew is not "obliged?" Beginning in contemporary times, we can trace the idea back to the second century A.D. This is not to claim that the idea originated then. We simply assert that it existed by then and that we have no clear evidence before that. Since we cannot logically assume that the idea arose out of nothing, we assume that the principle had a prior existence.

In light of the above reasoning, it seems not illogical to postulate the existence of a polarity. If the word "cult" or "liturgy" may be used in the broadest possible sense as "the acting out of something religious," it seems that perhaps we were dealing in the Old Testament with two remote liturgies. Even at this juncture we can name them, "a cult of judgment" and "a cult of non-judgment." The idea of a polarity is attractive. So common are polarities in myth that Levi-Strauss concluded that to find the existence of X is to prove the existence of non-X. In this case, the existence of the polarity has turned out to be better founded than that. The following pages will make this clear.

In reading the *P*-narrative in its present form a number of features seem terribly clear. The first is that the narrative is almost totally devoid of "obligation" or references to "obligation." The few references to "sin" are vague and abstract. There is little in the *P*-narrative that is "shocking or disedifying." If one compares an occasional *P* passage with one of the other sources, this fact becomes very clear. For example, the "shocking and disedifying" account of Sodom is reduced in the *P*-narrative to a single line: When God destroyed the cities of the plain, he thought of Abraham and he rescued him and Lot (*Gen.* 19:29). In fact, if one re-reads the *P*-narrative and searches for "obligation," a surprising result ensues. There are really only two forms of "obligation" hinted at. One of them is fairly directly spelled out: "The man-child who is not circumcised shall be cut off from his people. He has violated the covenant!" (*Gen.* 17:14). This stern insistence on circumcision is interesting to one who has read the entire *P*-narrative a number of times and has found the general approach to be that of a religion which is free of obligation.

There is one further reference to something which smacks of obligation. When the marriage of Esau with a foreigner takes place, the commentator notes "this was a grief to Isaac and Rebecca" (*Gen.* 26:35). Later the mother of Jacob begins to fear that the same thing may happen to Jacob, and she sighs, "If Jacob should take a wife from among strangers then what is my life worth to me?" (*Gen.* 27:46). It is difficult not to see here a remark which is aimed at a special audience, the pubescent male. He is being taught, in preparation for the rite of circumcision, that he has at least two obligations standing relatively soon before him. One is to submit to circumcision. The other is to defer to the wishes of the community in his choice of a wife.

These two "obligations" stand out because the rest of the narrative is so free of obligation. It reveals the kind of religion that is generally presented to children. A recurrent picture is that of the old patriarch on his deathbed blessing his children. The youngest of the children present at the scene eventually grows to a peaceful old age, and he lies in bed surrounded by his children and grandchildren. He blesses them and the burden of the blessing is this: transmit, carry on, be faithful.

The term "liturgy" means different things to different people. Part of the difficulty with the thesis being presented is that no clear evidence can be found in the *P*-narrative of a strict liturgical format with rubrics attached. There are partial evidences though. For example, in the *P*-narrative there are four places where the expression *be'eṣem hayyom hazzeh* occurs. And the expression does not otherwise occur in the Pentateuch. The expression, "in the bone of this day" (i.e., this *very* day) is interpreted to mean sundry things. The expressions are found in Genesis 7:13, Genesis 17:23 and 26, and Exodus 12:41. Each of the places involves a commandment of the Lord. "On this very day" Noah enters the ark at the Lord's behest (*Gen.* 7:13). "On this very day" Abraham circumcises Ishmael his son (*Gen.* 17:23), and is himself circumcised along with all the men of his household (*Gen.* 17:26), and "On this very day" the Israelites leave Egypt in answer to the word of the Lord (*Ex.* 12:41). Is there a further common denominator? Is it possible that we have primitive forms of what came to be "cultic re-presentation"—the sacramental making present of something that is historically past but effectively in the here and now? Sacramental re-presentation grew more complex in later theologies. It is possible to retroject some of that complexity or profundity into an earlier age. Could it be that sacramental re-presentation had its origins, at least partially, in child's play—the joy that the small child takes in pretending and in so making the past present? Is the expression, "on this very day" a fuller form of the sacramental "now" which we mentioned in an earlier chapter—the voice which spoke in the past but echoes even "now" that we may hear it? In the context, this reasoning seems fairly logical. The child, with religious encouragement, begins in the simple world of make-believe to re-enact the commands of the Lord. He enters the ark with Noah.

He leaves Egypt with his fathers. Having been so prepared, he
submits to the one command of the Lord which actively binds
him now, and he endures the painful rite of adolescent circumcision—possibly after having rehearsed somehow the circumcision of the adolescent Ishmael.

Some authors have seen in the rainbow legend of the *P*-nar-
rative (*Gen.* 9:12-17) an evidence for the use of this narrative in
the teaching of very young children. (One writer says "pre-
schoolers.") The reasoning is this: The rainbow in the sky is so
striking to someone who has never consciously looked at it
before (which would be the case with the very young), that it
could easily be the beginning of a primitive catechesis. "Why is
the pretty rainbow in the sky? Well, long ago men did very bad
things, and God had to punish them severely. Even though
they deserved it, God felt bad about it afterwards, and he
promised that he would never do it again. And as a reminder. . . ." One difficulty with the theory which supposes
that the audience of the *P*-narrative is very young is that it also
places the composition of the narrative late in Old Testament
history, in exilic or post-exilic times. By that time, Hebrew education of the very young had become quite stern. The attractive features of the writing, perhaps designed to appeal to a
young (or very young) audience, seem a bit out of place in what
was already becoming a very demanding pedagogy.

The logic of the *P*-source requires more than a young boy
could follow. For example, in ancient Arab legend the rainbow
in the sky was not an arbitrary symbol ("See the pretty colors
in the sky. . . ."). The semitic root for "rainbow" and "bow" is
is one and the same word. The bow as military weapon resem-
bles the bow in the heaven. Ancient Arab legend (flowing from
the same ancient Near Eastern Semitic world) saw the bow in
the sky as the weapon of the "arrow-shooting god." His wrath
now assuaged, he has therefore hung the mighty weapon in the
sky as a sign that he is no longer angry. The inner logic of this
perhaps demands a slightly older child as audience, although
we shall not press this one point.

A further argument is the absence of the decalogue in the *P*-
narrative. The *P*-legal has very detailed cultic laws that flow

from the Sinai experience, but the entire experience in the *P*-narrative is summed up in Exodus 31:18, "And the Lord (when he had finished speaking with him) gave Moses tablets of *edut* which were written on with God's finger." This is a reference to the tablets sometimes translated as the tablets of the law. But the force here is quite different. What then is *edut*?

The argumentation here is complex (and quite essential to the thesis) but shall be only briefly summed up. *Edut* in this place—as often elsewhere in the Old Testament—means "tradition." Even when the *P*-narrative deals with "obligation" material, such as the tablets of Sinai, it receives them into its own context. And the material received is changed significantly. The tablets of "the law" are described as the tablets of "tradition," because for the *P*-narrative, the only obligation other than circumcision is the obligation of transmission—handing on, being faithful to what one was taught.

Was there any reason why we should have gone looking for a children's liturgical narrative in the first place? There was a fairly good *a priori* reason. The Hebrew world is obsessed with survival as a common unity, not with the survival of individuals but with the survival of *Israel*. It is difficult to imagine the Hebrew world ignoring its young in religious services as did so many of her contemporaries. The Hebrew religion is very much obligation-oriented. But there is, as we have shown, some evidence that the young are not bound or obliged. If we want to find out how the young were instructed, would it not be reasonable to go looking for a fairly complete source in the Hebrew bible that had everything but obligation?

But there is also one *a posteriori* argument in favor of a children's narrative. In the book of Joshua (4:6 and 4:21) we read the following: "In days to come when your children ask, 'What do these stones mean?' [the priests had set twelve stones up in place across a brook] you shall explain that the Jordan was dry when Israel crossed over and that the Lord dried up the waters in front of you just as the Lord your God did at the Red Sea. . . ." It is difficult not to see here a reference to a narrative coupled with liturgy, a reciting or reading of words coupled with the acting out of a march across those stones, possibly coupled with the phrase *be'eṣem hayyom hasseh.* Now if one could only find a description in the *P*-source of a crossing of a body of water which is introduced by a question, our thesis would be very strong indeed. On the other hand, if such a passage could be found, maybe the thesis would be too easy to prove and would have long since been proven.

Where can we look for proof? There is a little narrative in Exodus 14:15-18, 21-23, 26, 28-29. It is a simple and graphic description of Moses leading the Hebrew people across unspecified waters. It is dramatic and replete with rubrics—"raise high your staff, stretch out your hand."

Perhaps the parallel between Exodus 14 and the passages in Joshua 4 may seem strained. It is not. Each passage deals clearly with the wonderous crossing of water under inspired leadership. There is evidence of a liturgical version of each, complete with rubrics: "stretch out your arm" (*Ex.* 14:16); "set up these stones" (*Josh.* 4:3). (The stones make the litrugical procession possible.) Finally, some confusion reigns in the rest of the Joshua passage as to whether Moses or Joshua is the leader. That points to an earlier version, since the thrust of the book of Joshua is that Moses is dead. In the Exodus version, Moses is clearly the leader.

In an absolutely ideal order, as we noted, the Exodus passage would have been introduced by the question: "What mean these stones?" It is not. Instead there is a question from the Lord: "What means this clamor?" Did two questions merge here? Was there a conflation or fusion of the two questions *mah tiṣ'aq 'eli* ("what means this cry to me?") and *mah ha'abenim* ("what mean these stones?")? We do not know. It is clear that the remainder of this little section in Exodus does deal precisely with the answer to the question posed by Joshua 4:6 and 4:21. Moreover, it is done with simplicity and dramatic detail, complete with rubrics, which would make it a good example of a "children's liturgy" in kernel.

There is one argument in favor of the conflation of the two questions which is not easily dismissed. It comes from a relatively new movement in biblical scholarship called *structuralism*. The structuralists give great emphasis to the vitality of the text itself, almost independent of history. For structuralists the primary concern of the biblical scholar should be the "deep structure"—the unexpressed unconscious idea which generates a variety of "surface structures."

For these scholars the "deep structure" has a powerful dynamic of its own. They would say a conflation like the one we have mentioned is possible not because the Hebrew words are alike in meaning or in sound (they are not), but because they could be reduced to the same "deep structure"—a necessary question which introduces an acted-out catechetical liturgy.

It is far too late in this book to get into a serious discussion about structuralism. But I think we can see even on a superficial level that the two questions found in Exodus and Joshua serve the same function. First there is a question, then there is dramatic activity coupled with rubrics. So the passages are quite similar.

Finally, if there was any teaching done in the ancient Hebrew world, one should look for it in a "liturgical" setting of some kind. The great German scholar, Julius Wellhausen, wrote long ago, "Hebrew priests are the pillars of the religious establishment, not because they sacrifice but because they teach." It is true that sacrifice is one aspect of cult, but another is drama. The priest who was both sacrificer and teacher would tend to teach in a liturgical setting. It seems a bit churlish to demand much more of the Exodus 14 passage than that which we have offered: a relationship to Joshua 4:6 and 4:21, the possibility of a conflated introductory question, the dramatic rubrics, and the detailed answer to the question (of Joshua 4:6), with a brief dramatic description of waters crossed.

In writing down this argument, much has been left out. It is hoped that the preceding pages are enough to make clear to the reader the high likelihood that there is a children's religious narrative in ancient Old Testament times, possibly in a liturgical setting, and that there is a relationship between the *P*-narrative we presently have—with its obligation-free religion—and the existence of that earlier children's liturgical narrative.

As an interesting illustration the following might be used. There is a chapter in a book *Myth, a Symposium* (Bloomington, 1958) by Ms. Dorothy Eggan entitled "The Personal Use of

Myth in Dreams." She writes of a "children's liturgy" found among the Hopi Indians. She describes it as an effective substitute for theater, church, and school. Although she does not use the term "sacramental re-presentation" she speaks of the learning process which takes place in an *emotionally charged atmosphere* which tends to *fuse reality and fantasy* (her italics). As a result of this dramatic learning, the Hopi child conforms to society's expectations.

Psalm 132:12 speaks of the good things that the Lord will do for David's sons if they guard "the covenant which I shall give them and the *edut* (testimony) which I shall teach them." Hebrew parallelism is not always simple. At least in the light of all that has been written until now, it is hard to dismiss here an allusion to a dual type of ancient Hebrew religion: faithfulness to the covenant, as witnessed through observance of the stipulations (the decalogue) by adults, and faithfulness to the *edut* learned even as a child and "taught," in this case at least, by the Lord.

The Cult of Judgment

This portion of the chapter shall be treated more briskly. For one thing, it remains largely in the realm of hypothesis. While a cult of judgment in the sense of "trial by ordeal" is fairly easy to document in the later written Old Testament, it is not easy to find in the Old Testament the cult of judgment with which we are concerned and which, I intuit, lies behind some of the older forms of the Hebrew scriptures. There are extrabiblical arguments which can be detailed. One of them, the activity of *Dan'el*, we have seen already. The argumentation from the Ugaritic material and other ancient traditions is stronger than simply argumentation from the common milieu of the Old Testament. The Ugaritic religious material is common to those "guild priests" who roamed through Canaan and came eventually into the employ of David and the service of his God. To find any evidence for a "cult of judgment" in the Ugaritic material is to find probability for the existence of something similar in Old Testament composition.

Arguing from "comparative religion" has something to offer. The Babylonian-Assyrian world that is common to the world of the Old Testament is preoccupied with the heavenly activity of judging. The common Akkadian motif has the god entrusting to the king a set of laws and the power to interpret them. But heavenly activity demands a cultic correspondence on earth.

One nineteenth century German writer used an argument from comparative religions quite differently. He was concerned not with religions that were contemporaneous with Israel but with certain common religious dynamics that were universal and to be found throughout a wide span of religious history. He compared, for example, the writing of Deuteronomy to the composition of the Icelandic *Grágás*. This material was composed by oral pilgrim judges, empowered to make decisions by the society in which they lived. Once these decisions were made they were formulated into principles—resulting in a kind of law-code. August Klostermann's work was not highly regarded at the time that he wrote. It was only with the work of Parry and Lord (mentioned in earlier chapters) that Klostermann became suddenly respectable. If Yugoslavian oral poets writing in 1930 were using the same techniques as ancient Semitic poets, it seemed not so absurd to accept that Icelandic poetry of the *Grágás* period was formulated through the same dynamic that produced Deuteronomy.

Another link in our logical chain was produced by the brilliant modern Israeli writer Moshe Weinfeld. The standard opinion of *JEDP* is that they were written over a long time. Weinfeld notes that this need not be so, that P and D were chronologically simultaneous but written for different audiences. This, of course, is what we have been saying all along about the judgment-source (for adults) and the non-judgment source (for adolescents). One can make a clearer case for the existence of a judgment *source* than for a judgment *cult*. One of the few suasive arguments for the cult theory has already been noted: There is need for motivation to accept difficult laws or life-modes. The *Grágás* clearly used some kind of priestly proclamation to enforce its decrees; Ms. Eggan cites the "emotionally charged atmosphere" of a children's liturgy that makes inevitable for the children the acceptance of social styles; we have similarly suggested that *Dan'el*, the judge of God, did indeed judge on the threshing floor, because that placed him in a cultic situation where his judgments might be accepted. But as valuable as the preceding arguments may be, some persons may feel that they are a long way from the Old Testament itself. Is there any Old Testament evidence that may be cited for the remote form of the "judgment-cult" of which I am speaking? Perhaps the strongest evidence is for the texts which refer to the activity at *Massah* (*Ex.* 17:7, *Deut.* 6:16, 9:22, 33:8, *Ps.* 95:8) and *Meribah* (*Ex.* 17:7, *Num.* 20:13, 20:24, 27:14, *Deut.* 33:8, *Ps.* 81:7, 106:32). Common opinion has made these references fairly "late." This is open to another opinion. If all these passages are read carefully, what do we find?

The Hebrew words themselves *Massah* (testing) and *Meribah* (dispute) point to some sort of contention. The texts contradict themselves on whether the dispute is between Moses and the people (*Ex.* 17:2), the people and God (*Deut.* 6:16), or Moses and God (*Deut.* 33:8 and *Num.* 20:24). Moreover there are contradictions on the mode of the dispute—what was being argued about, as well as who was doing the arguing. There is a possibility that *Massah* and *Meribah* are related to the *Marah* incident dealing with "bitterness of water" (*Ex.* 15:23). Can something be concluded from all of the above?

It is difficult to see how these contradictions are compatible with the "later" origin of these incidents. Confusion on very fundamental details as to who disputed with whom over what (and this after all in a "disputed account") would seem only to point to some incident or legend in remote antiquity which has become garbled in transmission. Again, is there a universal dynamic to which the *Massah* and *Meribah* accounts can be related?

Wellhausen spoke of the waters of *Meribah* as the "waters of ordeal" and saw allusion here to a process of testing, of discerning right or wrong between two individuals. The "water-or-deal" is common enough in later Hebrew writing, but in the ancient Mediterranean world there were very old antecedents.

In the *Iliad* Achilles wrestles with the river and is judged the victor. For some students of the Old Testament, something similar underlies the Jacob account in Genesis 32:22-25. In the version we have, the wrestling has been separated from the crossing of the river. In an earlier version, this may not have been so. The crossing was made possible by Jacob's victorious wrestling. It is at least interesting to note that this story—even its present form—is found outside the *P*-narrative and thus, according to our hypothesis, part of the judgment polarity. The Ugaritic material uses the divine name, Judge River, *špṭ nhr*. Against this backdrop, the meaning of that epithet is fairly easy to see. Remember the hypothesis we started with: A cult of non-judgment and a cult of judgment, one for children and one for adults, and both of them flowing together at a later time. How well have we done? Obviously the answer to that question lies not with the author but with the more learned readers of these pages. Still, a few suggestions can be made. The non-judgment source seems to hold together fairly well, even in this stage of our writing. We have a locus—the *P*-narrative—and a number of aspects in that locus that seem to be explicable through our hypothesis and only through our hypothesis. In the judgment half of the hypothesis, many problems remain at this juncture. We do not have a demonstrated locus. It is tempting to look for a *Vorlage* (a hidden earlier version) in the present Deuteronomy. Klostermann's parallel between the *Grágás* and an earlier Deuteronomy gives us courage to continue the search. But at this writing that is what we are doing. We are still searching.

One difficulty surely arises for all readers. If the above is true, how did the dynamic end? What caused the judgment-source and the non-judgment source to blend into one? Obviously, we do not know with any degree of certainty. We have hypothesized that at least some of the stipulations which grew into the decalogue had their origins in principles derived from a cult of judgment. This does not eliminate the need for discussing the "Sinai experience." Something happened there that was so dynamic that it colored all subsequent Israelite history. Did it simply blot out the primitive cult of judgment which had given rise to pre-Sinai stipulations? Did the Sinai event make all prior happenings forgettable experiences, to survive only in vestiges with confused references to *Massah, Meribah,* and *Marah?* Did the growth into a covenantal community make it impossible even for children to grow up without being "obligation-oriented" from their earliest years, so that the non-judgment cult survives only in a single source? There may be another explanation. In passages such as 2 Samuel 7:14, even the sacral king is seen as but a child before God his Father who will chastise him as father chastises a son who misbehaves. Perhaps, with the acceptance of sacral kingship, Israel came to see all men as mere children in the eyes of God, and grew uncomfortable with liturgies which separated adults and children. Our honest inability to answer the above questions with any degree of certitude should not detract from what we have done. For reasons which were explained in earlier chapters, we have had confidence in the idea of oral composition of early strata of the Old Testament. It is almost inevitable that we are unable to show all the seams that lie hidden in a work composed over such a long period of time. If the seams were not very well hidden, their unity would have collapsed long since. Bernard Anderson, in his translation *A History of Pentateuchal Traditions* (Prentice-Hall, 1972), attributes to Gunkel and Dilthey the following view of exegesis: "Exegesis is not a science but an art in which the critic with sensitivity and imagination seeks to 're-create' the situations in life of the people which find expression in literary works."

In H. A. Hodges' work *Wilhem Dilthey: An Introduction* (London: 1944), he makes the point that the skilled reader can recreate or reexperience those very life processes which led to the printed page. "In the operation of understanding itself, the life-process is reversed." A centuries' long progression led to a given text. By contemplating the text long enough we can come not only to know the meaning of these lines, but can reexperience the life-process which produced them.

For some persons this process will look much too subjective. They should be reminded however that the Old Testament is not a volume of empirical science, but a work of art.

And here we stop. It is with the fear that this chapter (and perhaps much of the book) has "fallen between two chairs" as the cliché has it. Learned colleagues will be distressed that more documentation was not offered. Younger readers may be weary that I offered as much argumentation as I did.

Still these pages, even in their present form, have something to offer each group. Colleagues have at least had interests stirred and provocation roused. Other readers may have been given an insight into the joys of those who heed Merlyn's advice.

SELECTED READINGS

Colossians 1:24   Isaiah 43:18f   Genesis 19:29
Mark 14:21   Isaiah 40:13   Genesis 17:14
Mark 14:49   Jeremiah 23:18   Genesis 7:13
                         Jeremiah 23:22   Genesis 17, 23, 26
CHAPTER 13   1 Kings 18:21   Exodus 12:41
                         Jeremiah 6:27   Genesis 9:12-17
Amos 8:2   Luke 13:33   Joshua 4:6
Ezekiel 7:2-3   Mark 6:4   Joshua 4:21
Hosea 1:9   Exodus 17:2
Jeremiah 12:7-8   **CHAPTER 14**   Deuteronomy 6:16
Isaiah 7:3   Numbers 20:24
Isaiah 14:1   1 Kings 22:10   Genesis 32:22-25

EXTENDED READINGS

Ch. 2-4: Book of Genesis (with special attention to ch. 12-36)
Ch. 5:   Book of Exodus (with special attention to ch. 1-20:21, ch. 24,
         and ch. 32-34)
Ch. 6:   Book of Deuteronomy
Ch. 7:   Book of Leviticus; Book of Jonah
Ch. 8:   Book of Joshua; Book of Judges
Ch. 9:   2 Samuel 2-8; 1 Kings 1-11; Psalms 48, 79, 122
Ch. 10: Psalm 119; Book of Proverbs; Book of Ecclesiastes
Ch. 11: Psalms 72, 89, 110; 2 Samuel 6-7; 1 Kings 3, 8; 2 Kings 22-23
Ch. 12: Isaiah 40-55
Ch. 13: Jeremiah 1-33
Ch. 14: P-source as listed in appendix

Appendix

Priestly, Jahwist, Elohist, and Deuteronomist
Sources in the Pentateuch
Analytical Outline of the Pentateuch

Appendix

A. THE BOOK OF GENESIS

	P	J	E	Other
1. *Urgeschichte*				
Creation story	1 : 1–2 : 4a			
Paradise story		2 : 4b–3 : 24		
Cain and Abel		4 : 1–16		
Cainite genealogy		4 : 17–26		
Genealogy, Adam to Noah	5 : 1–28	5 : 29		
	5 : 30–32			
The sons of God		6 : 1–4		
The Flood[1]				
Prologue		6 : 5–8		
Story	6 : 9–22			
		7 : 1–2		
		[7 : 3a]		
		7 : 3b–5		
	7 : 6	7 : 7		
	7 : 11	7 : 16b		
		[7 : 8–9]		
		7 : 10		
		7 : 12		
	7 : 13–16a			
	[7 : 17a]	7 : 17b		
	7 : 18–21	7 : 22–23		
	7 : 24			
	8 : 1, 2a	8 : 6a		
		8 : 2b, 3a		
	8 : 3b–5	8 : 6b		
	8 : 7	8 : 8–12		
	8 : 13a	8 : 13b		
	8 : 14–19			
Epilogue		8 : 20–22		
	9 : 1–17			
Noah's curse, blessing		9 : 18–27		
	9 : 28–29			
Table of nations	10 : 1–7	10 : 8–19		
	10 : 20	10 : 21		
	10 : 22–23			

[1] This analysis of the Flood Story agrees substantially with that of Gerhard von Rad, *Genesis*, The Old Testament Library (Philadelphia: Westminster Press, 1961). Noth omits the bracketed passages from his analysis.

	P	J	E	Other
	10 : 24[2]	10 : 25–30		
	10 : 31–32			
Tower of Babel		11 : 1–9		
Genealogy, Shem				
to Abraham	11 : 10–27	11 : 28–30		
	11 : 31–32			

2. *Patriarchal History*

ABRAHAM CYCLE (12 : 1–25 : 18)

	P	J	E	Other
Call of Abraham		12 : 1–4a		
	12 : 4b-5	12 : 6–9		
Abraham, Sarah in				
Egypt		12 : 10–13 : 1		
Separation from Lot		13 : 2–5		
	13 : 6	13 : 7–11a		
	13 : 11b-12	13 : 13–18		
Abraham's victory				Gen. 14 (special source)
Covenant with				
Abraham		15 : 1–2*		[Noth: first part of 15: 1b is E]
			15 : 3a	
		15 : 3b–4	15 : 5	
		15 : 6*–12	15 : 13–16	[Von Rad assigns
		15 : 17–21		15: 6 to E]
Ishmael's birth	16 : 1a	16 : 1b–2		
	16 : 3	16 : 4–14*		[Noth: 16:9–10 is redactional]
	16 : 15–16			
Covenant of				
circumcision	17 : 1–14			
The promise of a son	17 : 15–27			
Impending fate of				
Sodom				
The Lord's visit		18 : 1–16		
The Lord's				
monologue		18 : 17–19		
Dialogue with				
God		18 : 20–33		

[2] Noth: 10: 24 may be a harmonizing addition to connect Gen. 10: 22 (P) with the inserted material in 10: 25ff.

	P	J	E	Other
Sodom's destruction, Lot's deliverance		19 : 1–28		
	19 : 29			
Lot's daughters		19 : 30–38		
Abraham, Sarah in Gerar		20 : 1a	20 : 1b–18	
Isaac's birth, Ishmael's banishment	21 : 1b–5		21 : 6	
		21 : 7	21 : 8–21	
Abimelech of Gerar			21 : 22–34	
The testing of Abraham			22 : 1–19	
Nahor's descendants		22 : 20–24		
Purchase of a burial place	23 : 1–20			
A bride for Isaac		24 : 1–67		
Children by Keturah		[25 : 1–4]		
		25 : 5–6		
Abraham's death	25 : 7–11a	25 : 11b		
Ishmael's descendants	25 : 12–17			25 : 18, gloss

JACOB CYCLE (25 : 19–36 : 43)

	P	J	E	Other
Birth of Esau, Jacob	25 : 19–20	25 : 21–26a		
	25 : 26b	25 : 27–34		
Isaac stories		26 : 1–33		
	26 : 34–35			
The stolen blessing		27 : 1–45		
Jacob's exile to Aram	27 : 46– 28 : 9			
Jacob's dream at Bethel		28 : 10	28 : 11–12	
		28 : 13–16	28 : 17–18	
		28 : 19	28 : 20–22	
Jacob's arrival in Aram		29 : 1–14		
Marriage to Leah and Rachel		29 : 15–30		

	P	J	E	Other
Jacob's children		29 : 31–35		
			30 : 1–3	
		30 : 4–5	30 : 6	
		30 : 7–16	30 : 17–19	
		30 : 20–21	30 : 22–23	
		30 : 24		
Jacob's wealth		30 : 25–43		
Jacob's flight, covenant with Laban		31 : 1	31 : 2	
		31 : 3	31 : 4–16	
		31 : 17		
	31 : 18			
		31 : 19a	31 : 19b	
		31 : 20–23	31 : 24–25a	
		31 : 25b	31 : 26	
		31 : 27	31 : 28–29	
		31 : 30a	31 : 30b	
		31 : 31	31 : 32–35	
		31 : 36a	31 : 36b–37	
		31 : 38–40	31 : 41–45	
		31 : 46–49	31 : 50	
		31 : 51–53a	31 : 53b–55	
The angel of Mahanaim			32 : 1–2	
Preparations to meet Esau		32 : 3–13a	[32 : 13b–21]	
Jacob's wrestle at Penuel		32 : 22–32		
The meeting with Esau		33 : 1–3	33 : 4–5	
		33 : 6–7	33 : 8–11	
		33 : 12–17		
Jacob's arrival at Shechem	33 : 18a	33 : 18b		
			33 : 19–20	
The rape of Dinah		34 : 1–31		
Jacob's return to Bethel			35 : 1–5	
	35 : 6		35 : 7–8	
	35 : 9–13		35 : 14	
	35 : 15			
The birth of Benjamin			35 : 16–20	
Jacob's sons		35 : 21–22a		
	35 : 22b–26			

	P	J	E	Other
Isaac's death	35 : 27–29			
Edomite lists	36 : 1–14			36: 15—43 (addition to P)

HISTORY OF JACOB'S SONS (chapters 37–50)

	P	J	E	Other
Joseph's dream and consequences	37 : 1–2	37 : 3a	37 : 3b	
		37 : 4–21	37 : 22–24	
		37 : 25–28	37 : 29–36	
Interlude: Judah and Tamar		38 : 1–30		
Temptation of Joseph		39 : 1–23		
Joseph interprets dreams in prison		40 : 1	40 : 2–23	
Interpretation of Pharaoh's dreams; Joseph's elevation			41 : 1–33	
		41 : 34a	41 : 34b, 35a	
		41 : 35b	41 : 36–40	
		41 : 41–45		
	41 : 46a			
		41 : 46b	41 : 47–48	
		41 : 49	41 : 50–54	
		41 : 55–57		
The brothers' first trip to Egypt			42 : 1a	
		42 : 1b	42 : 2–3	
		42 : 4–5	42 : 6–7	
		42 : 8–11a	42 : 11b	
		42 : 12	42 : 13–26	
		42 : 27–28a	42 : 28b–37	
		42 : 38		
The brothers' second trip		43 : 1–34		
The testing of the brothers		44 : 1–34		
The recognition		45 : 1	45 : 2–3	
		45 : 4–5a	45 : 5b–15	
		45 : 16–28		
Jacob's settlement in Egypt			46 : 1–5a	
		46 : 5b		
	46 : 6–27	46 : 28–34		

	P	J	E	Other
Jacob before Pharaoh		47 : 1–5a 47 : 6b	47 : 5b, 6a 47 : 7–12	
Joseph's agrarian policy		47 : 13–26		
	47 : 27–28			
Blessing of Ephraim, Manasseh		47 : 29–31	48 : 1–2	
	48 : 3–6		48 : 7–22	
The Blessing of Jacob	49 : 1a			49: 1b–28 (special source; vs. 28 is a redactional link)
Jacob's death	49 : 29–33			
Jacob's burial		50 : 1–10a	50 : 10b–11	
	50 : 12–13	50 : 14		
Joseph's forgiveness and last days			50 : 15–26	

B. THE BOOK OF EXODUS[3]

1. *The Exodus from Egypt* (1 : 1–15 : 21)

	P	J	E	Other
The oppression	1 : 1–7 1 : 13–14	1 : 8–12		
The Hebrew midwives			1 : 15–21	
		1 : 22		
Moses' birth		2 : 1–10		
Moses' flight to Midian		2 : 11–22		
Moses' call Prologue	2 : 23*–25			[Noth: first part of 2 : 23a is J]
The burning bush		3 : 1–4a 3 : 5	3 : 4b 3 : 6	
The commission		3 : 7–8	3 : 9–12	
The divine Name			3 : 13–15	
A preview of events to come		3 : 16–22		
Signs		4 : 1–9		
Aaron as Moses' aide		4 : 10–16	4 : 17	

[3] See also Martin Noth's commentary, *Exodus*, The Old Testament Library (Philadelphia: Westminster Press, 1962), where the analysis outlined here is modified in part.

Appendix

	P	J	E	Other
Moses' return to Egypt				
Farewell to Jethro			4 : 18	
		4 : 19		
		4 : 20a	4 : 20b	
"Let my son go"		4 : 21–23		
Yahweh's attack upon Moses		4 : 24–26		
Meeting with Aaron		4 : 27–31		
Moses' demand and its consequences		5 : 1–6 : 1		
Another call of Moses	6 : 2–13			
The house of Levi	6 : 14–27			
Aaron as Moses' spokesman	6 : 28–7 : 7			
The plagues against Egypt				[Other scholars find E elements in chs. 7–10]
Introduction	7 : 8–13			
Plague of blood		7 : 14–18		
	7 : 19, 20aα	7 : 20, 21a		
	7 : 21b, 22	7 : 23–24		
Plague of frogs		7 : 25–8 : 4		
	8 : 5–7	8 : 8–15a		
	8 : 15aβb			
Plague of gnats	8 : 16–19			
Plague of flies		8 : 20–32		
Plague on cattle		9 : 1–7		
Plague of boils	9 : 8–12			
Plague of hail		9 : 13–35		
Plague of locusts		10 : 1–20		
Plague of darkness		10 : 21–29		
The Passover and the Exodus				
Announcement of final plague		11 : 1–8		
	11 : 9–10			
Institution of the Passover	12 : 1–20	12 : 21–23		12 : 24–27a (Dtr supplement)[4]
		12 : 27b		
	12 : 28			

[4] Otto Eissfeldt assigns this passage to his oldest source (L), while S. R. Driver assigns it to the old epic tradition (JE).

	P	J	E	Other
The final plague		12 : 29–36		
The Exodus		12 : 37–39		
	12 : 40–42			
Passover supplement	12 : 43–51			
Consecration of first-born; Unleavened Bread				13 : 1–16 (Dtr supplement)
Victory at the Reed Sea			13 : 17–19	
		13 : 20–22		
	14 : 1–4		14 : 5a	
		14 : 5b, 6	14 : 7	
	14 : 8–10*			[Noth: 14 : 10 has elements of J]
			14 : 11–12	
		14 : 13–14		
	14 : 15–18		14 : 19a	
		14 : 19b, 20		
	14 : 21–23	14 : 24	14 : 25a	
		14 : 25b		
	14 : 26	14 : 27aα		
	14 : 28–29	14 : 30–31		
The Song of Moses				15 : 1–19 (special source)
The Song of Miriam		15 : 20–21		

2. *The Beginning of the Wilderness Sojourn* (15 : 22–18 : 27)

	P	J	E	Other
First stations	15 : 22aα 15 : 27	15 : 22–25a		15 : 25b, 26 (Dtr supplement)
Quails and manna	16 : 1–3 16 : 6–27 16 : 32–35a	16 : 4–5 16 : 28–31 16 : 35b, 36		
Water from the rock	17 : 1	17 : 2 17 : 4–7	17 : 3	
Victory over Amalek		17 : 8–16		
Jethro's visit			18 : 1–27	

	P	J	E	Other
3. *The Sinai Covenant* (19 : 1–24 : 11)				
Introduction	19 : 1, 2a			
Encampment at the mountain		19 : 2b	19 : 3a	
Covenant invitation			19 : 3b–6*	[Noth: 19: 3b–9 is a Dtr supplement]
Response of the people		19 : 7–9(?)*		
Preparation of the people			19 : 10–11a*	[Noth: almost all of 19: 10–15 is J]
		19 : 11b–13		
			19 : 14–15*	
The theophany			19 : 16–17	
	19 : 18		19 : 19	
	19 : 20–25			
The Decalog			20 : 1–21	
The Covenant Code			20 : 22–	
			23 : 33*	[Noth: special source]
The covenant ceremony		24 : 1–2*		[Noth: 24: 1–2 is E]
			24 : 3–8*	[Noth: 24: 3–8 is a special source]
		24 : 9–11*		[Noth: 24: 9–11 is E]
4. *Cultic Instructions Given on Sinai* (24 : 12–31 : 17)				
Introduction			24 : 12–15a	
	24 : 15b– 25 : 9			
The Ark	25 : 10–22			
The Table	25 : 23–30			
The Lamps	25 : 31–40			
The Tabernacle	26 : 1–37			
The Altar and Court	27 : 1–21			
Priestly garments	28 : 1–43			
Installation of priests	29 : 1–46			
The altar of incense	30 : 1–10			
The census	30 : 11–16			

	P	J	E	Other
The water basin	30 : 17–21			
The holy oil	30 : 22–33			
On making incense	30 : 34–38			
The artisans	31 : 1–11			
Sabbath obser- vance	31 : 12–17			

5. *Apostasy and Covenant*
Renewal
(31 : 18–34 : 35)

	P	J	E	Other
The Golden Calf	31 : 18	32 : 1a 32 : 4b–6	32 : 1b–4a	
				32: 7–14 (Dtr supplement)
		32 : 15–20 32 : 25–35	32 : 21–24	
Yahweh's presence		33 : 1–23[5]		
Covenant renewal		34 : 1–28		
Moses' transfigura- tion		34 : 29–35		

6. *Execution of the Instructions*
Given in Chs. 25–31

	P
	35:1–39:43
Erection of the sanctuary	40 : 1–38

C. THE BOOK OF LEVITICUS

1. *Laws Dealing with Sacrifices* (1–7)

	Additions to P:
Burnt offerings	1: 1–17
Cereal offerings	2: 1–16
Peace offerings	3: 1–17
The sin offering	4: 1–5: 13
The guilt offering	5: 14–6: 7
Instructions to priests	6: 8–7: 38

2. *Consecration of Priests* (8–10)

Installation of priests
(see Ex. 29)   8 : 1–36

---

[5] Ch. 33 is problematic; Noth regards it as a "conglomeration" which perhaps was associated with J.

	P	J	E	Other
Beginning of Aaron's high priesthood	9 : 1–24			
Nadab and Abihu	10 : 1–20			

3. *Laws on Clean and Unclean* (11–15)   Additions to P:

	P	J	E	Other
Clean and unclean animals				11: 1–47
Purification after childbirth				12: 1–8
Diagnosis of leprosy				13: 1–59
Cleansing of leprosy				14: 1–32
Bodily discharges				15: 1–32

4. *Day of Atonement Ceremony*

16 : 1–34

5. *The Holiness Code* (17–26)   Additions to P:

	P	J	E	Other
Slaughter of animals				17: 1–16
Forbidden sexual relations				18: 1–30
The life of holiness				19: 1–37
Violation of theocratic rules				20: 1–27
Instructions to priests				21: 1–22: 25
Sacred calendar				23: 1–44
Priestly laws				24: 1–23
Sabbatical year, year of jubilee				25: 1–55
The Two Ways				26: 1–46

6. *Appendix on Religious Vows*   27: 1–34

D. THE BOOK OF NUMBERS

1. *Preparations for Departure* (1 : 1–10 : 10)

	P	J	E	Other
Census of the tribes	1 : 1–54			
Arrangement of the tribes	2 : 1–34			

	P	J	E	Other
Levites set apart	3 : 1–51			
A Levitical census	4 : 1–49			
Instructions to the people				5:1–6:21 (addition to P)
Offerings from tribal leaders	7 : 1–89			
Setting up the lamps	8 : 1–4*			[Noth: 8:1–4 is "an isolated piece"]
Consecration of the Levites	8 : 5–26			
Other events, instructions	9:1–10:10			

2. *The Sojourn at Kadesh-barnea*
   (10:11–21:13; see also Ex. 17–18)

	P	J	E	Other
Israel on the march	10 : 11–28			
Hobab, desert guide		10 : 29–32		
The Ark		10 : 33–36		
Israel's murmuring		11 : 1–35		

[In 11 : 16–17, 24–25, J preserves old tradition; form-critically the chapter is composite]

	P	J	E	Other
Miriam's punishment		12 : 1–16		
Reconnaissance of the land	13 : 1–17a	13 : 17b–20		
	13 : 21	13 : 22–24		
	13 : 25–26	13 : 27–31		
	13 : 32–33			
Murmuring and its consequences	14 : 1a	14 : 1b		
	14 : 2–3	14 : 4		
	14 : 5–10	14 : 11–25		
	14 : 26–38			
Abortive attack upon southern Canaan		14 : 39–45		
Cultic regulations				15:1–41 (addition to P)

Revolts against
   Moses [Here two stories are blended: one dealing with Korah, the other with Dathan and Abiram]

	P	J	E	Other
	16 : 1a	16 : 1b [to "took men"]		
	16 : 2–11	16 : 12–15		
	16 : 16–24	16 : 25–26		
	16 : 27a	16 : 27b–34		
	16 : 35–50			
Aaron's budding rod	17 : 1–13			
Duties of Aaronic priests and other Levites	18 : 1–32			
Defilement by a corpse				19: 1–22 (addition to P)
Water from the rock	20 : 1–13			

3. *The Journey from Kadesh via Transjordan* (20 : 14–27 : 23)

	P	J	E	Other
Departure from Kadesh			20 : 14–18	
		20 : 19–20	20 : 21	
Aaron's death		20 : 22a		
	20 : 22b–29			
The battle of Hormah		21 : 1–3		
The bronze serpent		21 : 4–9		
An old itinerary				21: 10–20 (fragments of tradition)
Victory over Sihon and Og			21 : 21–35	
Balak and Balaam				22: la (redactional)
	22 : 1		22 : 2–3a	
		22 : 3b–8	22 : 9–12	
		22 : 13–19	22 : 20	
		22 : 21–37	22 : 38	
		22 : 39–40		
The four oracles of Balaam			22:41–23:27	
		23 : 28	23 : 29–30	
		24 : 1–25		
Incidents of apostasy in Moab		25 : 1–5		
	25 : 6–18*⁶			

⁶Noth believes that 25: 6–18 is a secondary addition to the completed Pentateuch.

	P	J	E	Other
A second census of the tribes				26:1–65 (addition to P)
Inheritance of property by women				27:1–11 (addition to P)
Commissioning of Joshua	27:12–23			
4. *Various Cultic and Legal Matters* (28–36)				Additions to P
Offerings for various occasions				28:1–29:40
Vows made by women				30:1–16
Holy war against Midian				31:1–54
Allotment of land in Transjordan		32:1		32:2–15
		32:16		32:17–38
		32:39–42		
Israel's itinerary				33:1–49
Ideal boundaries of the promised land				34:1–29
Levitical cities, cities of refuge				35:1–34
Tribal property to be maintained intact				36:1–12

E. APPENDICES TO THE BOOK OF DEUTERONOMY (31:1–34:12)

	P	J	E	Other
Moses' final charge to Joshua and people				31:1–8 (Dtr)
Sabbatical covenant ceremony				31:9–13 (Dtr)
Joshua's commission		31:14–15, 23(JE)*		[Noth: 31:14–15, 23 is Dtr]
Yahweh's charge to Moses (introduction to Song of Moses)				31:16–22 (by the editor who inserted the Song [Dtr?])

	P	J	E	Other
The Law to be placed in the Ark				31:24–29 (Dtr)
The Song of Moses Introduction				31:30 (Dtr)
The Song				32:1–43 (special tradition)
Conclusion				32:44–47 (by the editor who inserted the Song [Dtr?])
Moses' impending death	32:48–52*			[Noth: 32:48–52 secondarily repeats Num. 27:12–14]
The Blessing of Moses				33:1–29 (special tradition)
Moses' death	34:1aα	[34:1b–5a(JE)]		
	[34:5b]	[34:6(JE)]		
	34:7–9	[34:10(JE)]		

NOTE: A good brief introduction to the literary, form-critical, and traditio-historical study of the Pentateuch is found in Walter Harrelson, *Interpreting the Old Testament*. See especially pp. 27–40 and the appendix, Table of Pentateuchal Sources, pp. 487–92.

A more technical introduction is found in Otto Eissfeldt, *The Old Testament: An Introduction*, pp. 155–248.

Index

(Foreign words are listed in English alphabetic order,
not where the Semitist might look for them.)

197